# HISTORIC
# HOUSES
# AND
# ROYAL PALACES
# ALMANAC

Published in association with
**The English Tourist Board**

**Eric Dobby Publishing**

Published by
ERIC DOBBY PUBLISHING
12 Warnford Road
Orpington
Kent BR6 6LW

First published in 1994

© Eric Dobby Publishing 1994

A catalogue record of this book is available from the British
Library

ISBN: 1-85882 028 6

Typeset in Times by Kevin O'Connor, Poole
Printed and bound in Great Britain by
BPC Hazell Books Ltd
A member of
The British Printing Company Ltd

# **Introduction**

England's royal palaces and historic houses, including its stately homes, are part of its heritage and exist throughout the country providing an almost limitless number of places to visit, explore and enjoy. Some have changed very little from when they were built; others are still family homes which have been added to over the generations; all provide a wonderful understanding of the rich history and heritage of England.

This guide contains a selection of some of the best locations open to the public. The palaces, stately homes and historic houses included represent some of the finest examples to be found in England with places to visit in virtually all areas of the country. They are in county sequence, enabling the reader to locate them easily and, if required, to ascertain their proximity to other locations. The sequence within county is not in strict alphabetical order, this enables the publisher to show on facing pages those examples which cover two pages. There is also an index to enable readers to select a location quickly.

Each entry is illustrated in colour and provides all the practical information needed to plan and enjoy a visit. A concise description mentions the history of the palace, stately home or historic house and gives information about any special, significant or important aspects. Information is also given on opening times, admission charges, parking availability, brief notes on local travel directions and notes on some special events. In addition there are details on the facilities available and access for visitors in wheelchairs. Whilst every effort has been made to ensure that the information given is correct, details can change. Some readers may therefore find it best to check certain details before visiting (using the telephone number) especially if they have special requirements or are going in a large group. The Publishers would like to express their thanks to Jane Collinson of the English Tourist Board, the National Trust, English Heritage and the staff at the many locations in the book who have helped in providing the information, details and photographs.

Indicates a National Trust property

Indicates an English Heritage property

Owner a member of the Historic Houses Association

# Contents (by order of county)

**Bold** figures refer to map, *Italic* to page in book

# Contents (by alphabetical order)

**Bold** figures refer to map, *Italic* to page in book

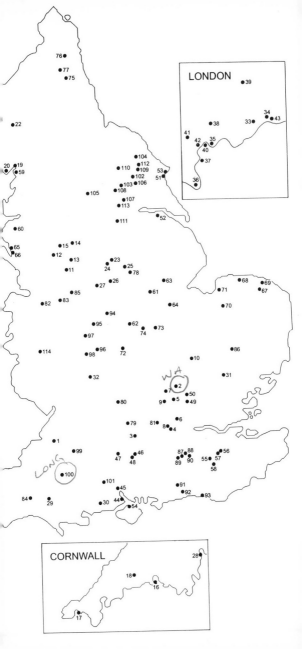

# Historic Houses

# and

# Royal Palaces

# DYRHAM PARK

*Near Chippenham, Avon SN14 8ER Tel: (0225) 891364*
*8m north of Bath; off A46; 2m S of M4, exit 18*

**Ownership:** The National Trust

**General Description:** At the foot of 263 acres of ancient parkland grazed by fallow deer and looking across to the Welsh Hills is William Blaythwayt's magnificent mansion. Blaythwayt was Secretary at War and Secretary of State to William III between 1691 and 1710. Little has changed in the rooms at Dyrham since he furnished them and the contents were recorded in his housekeeper's inventory.
The house is a marvellous reminder of the 17th century. Beyond it lies the naturalised formal garden.

**Open:** 26th March to 30th October, daily except for Thursday and Friday 12.00-5.30. Park open all year 12.00-5.30 except for Christmas Day.

**Admission:** £4.80, child £2.40; Park only £1.50, child 80p.

**Facilities:** Refreshments are served in the Orangery. Free car park near the house. Shop.

**Disabled Access:** Access is limited to the ground floor of the house, the Orangery and the terrace. Parking close to the house. Wheelchairs available.

**Additional information:** Picnics in the park. Dogs welcome on leads in designated areas but not in the deer park.

**Special Events:** Jazz Festival in July.

# WOBURN ABBEY

*Bedfordshire MK43 0TP Tel: (0525) 290666*
*On A4012; midway M1 exit 13 and A5 Hockliffe turn*

**Ownership:** Marquess of Tavistock

**General Description:** Set in the magnificent 3,000 acre Deer Park, Woburn Abbey provides a fascinating insight into England's architectural, cultural and historical heritage in which the same family have lived for over 350 years. It is a treasure house of paintings by many famous artists including Canaletto, Gainsborough, Rembrandt and Reynolds and there are numerous important pieces of furniture, silver and porcelain.

**Open:** 27th March to 30th October, Sunday & Bank Holidays 11.00-5.00, Monday to Saturday 11.00-4.00. Deer Park: Sunday & Bank Holidays 10.00-4.45, Monday to Saturday 10.00-4.30. 1st January to 26th March, Abbey Saturday and Sunday 11.00-4.00, Deer Park 10.30-3.45.

**Admission:** £6.50, child (12-16) £3.00. senior citizens/ student £5.50. Family tickets available. Park only: Car £5.00, M/cycles £2.00, others 50p.

**Facilities:** Free parking. The Flying Duchess Pavilion provides lunches and teas. Visitors may also visit the Antiques Centre, Woburn Pottery and the Abbey Shops. The Safari Park is approximately one mile away.

**Disabled Access:** Wheelchairs can be accommodated in the Abbey by prior arrangement. Toilets.

**Additional information:** Picnics in the Deer Park. Dogs welcome on leads in the park.

# BASILDON PARK

*Lower Basildon, Reading, Berks RG8 9NR*
*Tel: (0734) 843040*
*W side A329, 7m NW of Reading (M4 exit 12)*

**Ownership:** The National Trust

**General Description:** A classical 18th-century house by John Carr of York, in a beautiful setting overlooking the Thames Valley. The focal point of the interior is an unusual Octagon room. The house also contains fine plasterwork, important pictures and furniture and a decorative shell room. There is a small formal garden and woodland walks.

**Open:** 30th March to end October, Wednesday to Saturday 2.00-6.00, Sundays & Bank Holiday Mondays 12.00-6.00 (closed Good Friday and Wednesday following Bank Holidays). Grounds also open Saturday 12.00-6.00.

**Admission:** £3.50, Family £9.00; Grounds only £2.50, Family £6.00.

**Facilities:** Car parking. Teas available during opening hours with lunches also served on Saturday, Sunday and Bank Holiday Mondays.

**Disabled Access:** Garden, tea-room and shop accessible by wheelchair. Volunteer-driven buggy and stair climber in house.

**Additional information:** Picnic area by car park. National Trust shop. Dogs allowed on leads in grounds only.

**Special Events:** Annual Jazz Concert with fireworks in August.

# DORNEY COURT

*Windsor, Berkshire SL4 6QP Tel: (0628) 604638*
*M4 exit 7 then A4 and B3026*

**Ownership:** Mr & Mrs Peregrine Palmer

**General Description:** 'One of the finest Tudor manor houses in England,' *Country Life.* An enchanting, many-gabled house in pinkish brick of half-timber frame construction. The rooms are full of early 15th and 16th-century oak, beautiful 17th-century lacquer, 18th and 19th-century tables, family portraits, stained glass and needlework. Here Charles II came to enjoy the charms of Barbara Palmer, Countess of Castlemaine.

**Open:** Good Friday to Easter Monday: May, Sunday and Bank Holidays; June to September, Sunday, Monday and Tuesday, 2.00-5.30.

**Admission:** £3.50, child (over 9) £1.75.

**Facilities:** Car parking near house. Refreshments served.

**Disabled Access:** Very limited access.

**Additional information:** Pick Your Own Fruit from early June to late August. The Bressingham Plant Centre is part of the estate. Visitors can picnic near the house. Dogs are not allowed.

**Special events:** Regular gardening lectures and demonstrations at Bressingham Plant Centre.

# ASCOTT

*Wing, Nr Leighton Buzzard, LU7 0PS Tel: (0296) 688242
Midway Bicester & Thame – 2m W of Brill*

**Ownership:** The National Trust

**General Description:** The Anthony de Rothschild collection is housed in this charming house. There are fine pictures, French and English furniture and exceptional Oriental porcelain. The garden contains unusual trees, flower borders, naturalised bulbs, water-lilies and a topiary sundial.

**Open:** 12th April to 15th May & 1st to 30th September, Tuesday to Sunday 2.00-6.00. Garden only: 6th April & 18th May to 31st August, every Wednesday and last Sunday in each month 2.00-6.00.

**Admission:** £5.00; grounds only £3.00.

**Facilities:** Car park 220 yards from house.

**Disabled Access:** Access to ground floor only. Limited access to garden. Special parking by prior arrangement.

**Additional information:** No refreshments. Dogs allowed only in car park.

# CHENIES MANOR HOUSE

*Rickmansworth, Herts WD3 6ER Tel: (0494) 762888*
*A404, 2.5m W of M25 exit 18*

**Ownership:** A. F. MacLeod Matthews

**General Description:** This 15th to 16th-century semi-fortified manor house was built by Sir John Cheyne about 1460. Sir John Russell (later the first Earl of Bedford) made additions in 1526. Henry VIII and Elizabeth I, with their courts, were entertained here. The house contains contemporary furniture and tapestries and there are beautiful flower arrangements throughout. Special features include a reputed 'priest's hole' and underground passages. The house is surrounded by several gardens: a white garden, a sunken garden and an extensive Physic Garden. There is also a reconstructed penitential maze and a medieval well.

**Open:** April to October, Wednesday & Thursday, 2.00-5.00. Also open late Spring and August Bank Holidays 2.00-6.00.

**Admission:** £3.50, child (under 14) £1.75; gardens only £1.75.

**Facilities:** Home-made teas in the Garden Room. Shop selling dried flowers, herbs and other souvenirs. Doll Collection. There are regular exhibitions in the 13th-century crypt. Free parking.

**Disabled Access:** Unsuitable for wheelchairs.

**Additional information:** No dogs.

# CLAYDON HOUSE

*Middle Claydon, Buckingham MK18 2EY*
*Tel: (0296) 730349*
*14m NW of Aylesbury, signposted from A413, A421 & A41*

**Ownership:** The National Trust

**General Description:** The most perfect expression of Rococo decoration in England, a series of great rooms with wood carvings in the Chinese and Gothick styles of the 18th century. Relics of the Civil War and a museum with mementos of Florence Nightingale and the Verney family.

**Open:** April to end October, Monday, Wednesday, Friday, Saturday, Sunday 1.00-5.00.

**Admission:** £3.50, Family £9.00.

**Facilities:** Car parking close to front door. Tea room.

**Disabled Access:** All ground floor accessible. Gardens via 2 steps and ramps.

**Additional information:** Dogs allowed in park on lead.

**Special Events:** There are several concerts during the summer months.

# CLIVEDEN

*Taplow, Maidenhead, Berks SL6 0JA Tel: (0628) 605069*
*2m N of Taplow; M4 exit 7, M40 exit 4*

**Ownership:** The National Trust

**General Description:** Set on cliffs, 200 feet above the Thames. The present house, the third on the site, was built in 1851 by Sir Charles Barry and was once the home of Nancy, Lady Astor. It is now let as an hotel although three rooms are open to the public. The 375 acres of garden and woodland include a magnificent parterre, a water garden and miles of woodland walks with spectacular views of the Thames.

**Open:** April to October, Thursday and Sunday 3.00-6.00; Grounds March to end October, daily 11.00-6.00, November to December daily 11.00-4.00.

**Admission:** £3.80, family £9.50. House £1.00 extra.

**Facilities:** Car parking 400 yards from house. Tea room. Shop.

**Disabled Access:** Largely accessible. Wheelchair access to house with some steps.

**Additional information:** Dogs welcome in specified woodland but not in garden.

**Special Events:** There is an Open Air Theatre during the summer.

# WADDESDON MANOR

*Nr Aylesbury, Buckinghamshire HP18 0JH*
*Tel: (0296) 651211*
*6m NW of Aylesbury on A41, 11m SE of Bicester;*
*(M40 exit 7)*

**Ownership:** The National Trust

**General Description:** This magnificent French renaissance style chateau, designed by the French architect, Destailleru, was built by Baron Ferdinand de Rothschild in the 1870s as a showcase for his superb collection of French Royal furniture, Savonnerie carpets, Sèvres porcelain and great Masters (including Gainsborough, Reynolds and Dutch and Flemish masters of the 17th century). The manor is open again after three years of restoration. The landscaped gardens feature an elegant cast iron Rococo style aviary of exotic birds, built in 1889.

**Open:** 31st March to 16th October, Thursday to Saturday, Wednesday (July & August only), 1.00-6.00; Bank Holiday Sunday & Mondays 11.00-6.00.

**Admission:** £7.00, child (5-17) £5.50 (Additional charge of £1.00 on Sundays and Bank Holidays). Grounds £3.00, child £1.50, Family £7.50.

**Facilities:** Tea Room offering teas and lunches. Wine Cellars open to public and wine is for sale in Gift shop. Free car park for visitors.

**Disabled Access:** Ramp access and wheelchairs available. Shop, tearoom and most of grounds easy.

**Additional information:** Children's play area.

# WIMPOLE HALL

*Arrington, Royston, Herts SG8 0BW Tel: (0223) 207257*
*8m SW of Cambridge (A603), 6m N of Royston*

**Ownership:** The National Trust

**General Description:** The greatest country house in Cambridgeshire with sumptuous 18th and 19th-century public rooms including a Baroque chapel and the fine yellow drawing room designed by Soane. The Housekeeper's Room, Dry Store and Butler's Pantry give a fascinating glimpse of life 'below stairs'. There are acres of landscaped park, a gothic folly, grand avenues of trees and miles of walks. The gardens include parterres, the walled garden and pleasure gardens with thousands of daffodils.

**Open:** 26th March to 30th October, daily (except Monday and Friday), 1.00-5.00 and Bank Holiday Mondays; Bank Holiday Sundays and Mondays opens 11.00.

**Admission:** £4.50; joint ticket with farm £6.00.

**Facilities:** The Home Farm is a rare breeds centre. Children's Adventure Woodland and Wagon Rides. A variety of restaurants and tea rooms provide meals. Car parking. Picnic areas.

**Disabled Access:** 2 electric buggies plus wheelchairs. Please telephone before arrival to find out special arrangements.

**Additional information:** Dogs allowed in the park on leads. Picnic facilities adjacent to car park and at Home Farm.

**Special Events:** Opera and jazz concerts in June and July.

# LITTLE MORETON HALL

*Congleton, Cheshire CW12 4SD Tel: (0260) 272018*
*4m SW of Congleton, E side of A34*

**Ownership:** The National Trust

**General Description:** Surrounded by a moat and built round a cobbled courtyard, Little Moreton Hall is the most perfect example of a half-timbered house in the country. Few pieces of period furniture survive so the house is largely unfurnished. The wainscoted Long Gallery, early plasterwork, wall paintings, private Chapel and Great Hall are special features. Within the moated area the recreated formal Knot Garden would have been a typical feature of the 17th century.

**Open:** 26th March to end September, Wednesday to Sunday 12.00-5.30; Bank Holiday Monday 11.00-5.30 (Closed Good Friday); October, Saturday & Sunday 12.00-5.30.

**Admission:** Weekends and Bank Holidays £3.60, family £9.00. Other days £2.80, family £7.00.

**Facilities:** Coffee, lunch and afternoon teas in tea-room. Car park from 11.00 (£2.00 refundable).

**Disabled Access:** Wheelchair access to Great Hall, parlour, chapel, courtyard and garden. Wheelchair and electric mobility vehicle available.Toilets.

**Additional information:** Picnic lawn with tables. Dogs allowed in picnic lawn and car park only.

# ARLEY HALL

*Arley, Nr Northwich, Cheshire CW9 6NA Tel: (0565) 777353*
*Midway M56 exits 9 & 10, and M6 exits 19 & 20*

**Ownership:** The Hon Michael and Mrs Flower

**General Description:** Designed and built about 1840 by
George Latham, the Hall is an important example of
Victorian Jacobean style featuring a magnificent library and
historic family furniture, pictures and porcelain. The private
Chapel, built at the same date, was designed by Anthony
Salvin. The estate has been owned by the same family for
over 500 years. The gardens include a double herbaceous
border of 1846 design, a pleached Lime Avenue, an avenue
of shaped Quercus Ilex, yew hedges, walled gardens and a
herb garden.

**Open:** March to October, Tuesday to Sunday & Bank
Holidays, 12.00-4.30.

**Admission:** Grounds, Gardens and Chapel £2.80, child
£1.40; Hall (extra) £1.60, child 80p; farm £2.50.

**Facilities:** Lunches and light refreshments in the 16th-
century Tudor Barn. Gift shop.

**Disabled Access:** All parts accessible.

**Additional information:** Craft workshops (including cabinet
maker and wood turner), plant nursery and Stockley Farm – a
working farm with children's area. Tractor and trailer rides.
Dogs welcome on a lead.

# GAWSWORTH HALL

*Church Lane, Gawsworth, Macclesfield SK11 9RN*
*Tel: (0260) 223456*
*just off A536, 4m S of Macclesfield*

**Ownership:** Mr Tim Richards

**General Description:** This ancient manor house is a lovely 15th-century half-timbered building on a site dating back to Norman times. The ancient Fitton family chapel, first licensed in 1365, is still in use. The Hall itself contains pictures, furniture, sculpture and stained glass. Mary Fitton, probably the mysterious 'Dark Lady' of Shakespeare's sonnets, lived here whilst it is the site of the most famous duel fought in Britain between Lord Mohun and the Duke of Hamilton in 1712.

**Open:** 26th March to 9th October, daily 2.00-5.30.

**Admission:** £3.40, child (under 17) £1.70

**Facilities:** Free car park. Meals available in Pavilion Tea Room.

**Disabled Access:** No access to hall. Entry to grounds free for wheelchair visitors.

**Additional information:** Dogs not allowed. The Open Air Theatre is open from June to August.

**Special Events:** Open air theatre from July to August. Craft fairs.

# LYME PARK

*Disley, Stockport SK12 2NX Tel: (0663) 765035*
*A6 6m SE of Stockport, 9m NW of Buxton*

**Ownership:** The National Trust

**General Description:** A splendid example of 18th-century Palladian architecture by the Italian architect Giacomo Leoni, modified a century later by Lewis Wyatt. However it contains interiors of various periods including Elizabethan, Stuart, Georgian and Edwardian. Besides the collection of English furniture, there are family portraits (including works by Lely and Sargent) and an outstanding collection of English clocks presented by Sir Francis Legh. There is a 16 acre garden with formal parterres, herbaceous borders, an Edwardian Rose garden and a Victorian conservatory, as well as a moorland park of 1,300 acres with herds of red and fallow deer.

**Open:** 2nd April to 31st October, Saturday to Wednesday 1.30-5.00, Bank Holiday Mondays 11.00-5.00. Gardens 10.30-5.00.

**Admission:** Hall & Garden £2.50, Family £6.25, Garden only £1.00.

**Facilities:** Refreshments in tea room. Shop.

**Disabled Access:** Some parts of hall, garden and park and all tea room and shop accessible. Free booster scooter available. Please telephone for special arrangements. Toilets.

**Additional information:** Dogs allowed in park and gardens on leads.

**Special Events:** Viennese Evening with Firework Finale in August.

#  DUNHAM MASSEY HALL

*Altrincham, Cheshire WA14 4SJ Tel: 061-941 1025*
*3m SW of Altrincham; M6 exit 19, M56 exit 7/8*

**Ownership:** The National Trust

**General Description:** A fine 18th-century house with Victorian additions. George Booth, 2nd Earl of Warrington (1675-1758) rebuilt a decaying mansion, built the fine stable block and designed the parkland. The 30 rooms open include a Victorian billiard room and an Edwardian saloon. There is a vast kitchen and a large collection of silver, paintings and books, with souvenirs of the Grand Tour. The garden has a peaceful moat, an elegant red brick orangery and a working Jacobean mill. The formal parkland was not altered by the 18th-century designers and is a rare survival of its period.

**Open:** 2nd April to 30th October, Saturday to Wednesday 12.00-5.00; Park 11.00-5.30.

**Admission:** £4.50, child £2.00, family £11.00; house only £3.00 (child £1.50), garden only £2.50; park only £2.50 per car.

**Facilities:** Stables Restaurant serving lunch, teas and ice cream. Shop. Car park.

**Disabled Access:** Park and garden accessible, limited access to house and tea room. Please telephone for special arrangements. Toilets.

**Additional information:** Water-powerd Jacobean sawmill operates on Wednesday and Sunday. Picnic area. Dogs welcome on leads in deer park.

**Special Events:** Opera, theatre, music and other events.

# MOUNT EDGCUMBE HOUSE

*Cremyll, Torpoint, Cornwall PL10 1HZ Tel: (0752) 822236*
*B3247 off A374. By foot via Cremyll Ferry*

**Ownership:** City of Plymouth and Cornwall County Council.

**General Description:** A restored Jacobean and 18th-century house overlooking the lovely estuary of the Tamar and Plymouth Sound. Bombed during the last war it has been lovingly restored in great detail. The interior is in classical style with Doric columns and pilasters of blue marble. Much of the furniture, which is in period, has family associations. The whole design recreates its appearance in the 18th century. It is set in 800 acres overlooking Plymouth Sound with gardens that include the Earls and other formal Gardens and the landscaped park. Within the boundaries of the whole estate are fountains, temples, statues and summerhouses totalling over 50 listed buildings and structures.

**Open:** March 31st to October 31st, Wednesday to Sunday 11.00-5.30. Gardens and park open all year.

**Admission:** £3.00, concessions £2.15, child £1.50.

**Facilities:** Ample parking as well as pedestrian access by ferry from Plymouth. Orangery Restaurant. Shop and Exhibition Centre with regular art exhibitions.

**Disabled Access:** Access to whole house. Toilets.

**Additional information:** Picnic facilities. Dogs are welcome in the gardens and park but not the house or Earls Garden.

**Special events:** Plays, concerts and a cricket festival.

# ST MICHAEL'S MOUNT

*Marazion, Penzance, Cornwall TR17 0HT*
*Tel: (0736) 710507*
*S of A394 at Marazion by foot or ferry at high tide*

**Ownership:** The National Trust

**General Description:** This magical island is the jewel in Cornwall's crown, a national treasure which is a must for every visitor to the far West. The great granite crag which rises from the waters of Mount's Bay is surmounted by a 14th-century castle, modified over the centuries, and home of the St Aubyn family for over 300 years. The Mount's flanks are softened by lush sub-tropical vegetation and on the water's edge there is a harbourside community, an ancient trading place for tin and other Cornish goods which today features shops and restaurants.

**Open:** 30th March to 31st October, Monday to Friday 10.30-5.30.

**Admission:** £3.20, Family £8.00.

**Facilities:** Shops and restaurants.

**Disabled Access:** The island is inaccessible.

**Additional information:** No dogs allowed.

# LANHYDROCK

*Bodmin, Cornwall PL30 5AD Tel: (0208) 73320*
*2¹/₂m SE of Bodmin - follow signs from A30, A38 or B3268*

**Ownership:** The National Trust

**General Description:** Rooms reflecting Victorian comfort to maids' bedrooms, larders and the great kitchen. First built in the 17th century and largely rebuilt after a fire in 1881, the principal rooms all have beautifully worked plaster ceilings, including that of the Long Gallery magnificently illustrating Old Testament scenes. Through the crenellated gatehouse (1641) an idyllic walk down to the River Fowey at Respryn Bridge and back through the woods should not be missed.

**Open:** 30th March to 31st October daily except Monday (when House is closed) (Open Bank Holiday Mondays), 11.00-5.30 (5.00 in October).

**Admission:** £5.00; garden & grounds only £2.50.

**Facilities:** Refreshments available. Shop.

**Disabled Access:** Yes, via ramps and lift.

**Additional information:** Dogs allowed in park on leads.

# LEVENS HALL

*Kendal, Cumbria LA8 0PN Tel: (05395) 60321*
*5m S of Kendal on A6*

**Ownership:** C. H. Bagot

**General Description:** Amongst its many treasures this stone-built Elizabethan house has a fine collection of Jacobean furniture, paintings by Rubens, Lely and Cuyp, Cromwellian armour, portraits and miniatures. The earliest English patchwork (c.1708) is on display. The famous topiary garden, 300 years old in 1994, is one of the few remaining with its original design and many of its original trees.

**Open:** 3rd April to 30th September, daily except Friday and Saturday, 2.00-5.00.

**Admission:** £3.50, child £1.90; gardens only £2.20, child £1.10.

**Facilities:** Lunches and teas. Shop.

**Disabled Access:** House not accessible.

**Additional information:** There is a steam collection on show. Play and picnic area. No dogs.

# HOLKER HALL

*Cark-in-Cartmel, Near Grange-over-Sands,*
*Cumbria LA11, 7PL*
*Tel: (05395) 58328*
*B278 or B277; M6 exit 36 follow A590*

**Ownership:** Lord Cavendish of Furness.

**General Description:** The Hall has been building since the 18th century but much of its appearance today is of Victorian splendour and comfort. The interior has much fine furniture and many important paintings and drawings. The 25 acres of magnificent formal and woodland gardens have been classed as among the best in the world. There are many rare and beautiful plants and special features such as the limestone cascade.

**Open:** 1st April to 31st October, Sunday to Friday 10.30-4.30.

**Admission:** £5.75, child £3.25, Family £16.00; excluding House or Museum £4.75, child £2.85, Family £8.00; grounds £3.00, child £1.70.

**Facilities:** Car park. Café, Motor Museum, Adventure Playground and Gift Shop.

**Disabled Access:** Ramps for most areas. Toilets.

**Additional information:** Picnic areas in the Deer Park.

# MIREHOUSE HOUSE

*Keswick, Cumbria CA12 4QE Tel: (07687) 72287*
*3m N of Keswick on A591*

**Ownership:** John Spedding

**General Description:** The central part of the house was built in 1666 with Georgian Gothick additions in the 1790s and more 'modern' parts in the 19th century. The house has many literary associations with manuscripts and portraits of writers including Tennyson, Wordsworth, and Carlyle. The paintings include ones by Romney, Francesco Longhi and Constable. Listen to live piano music as you wander through the house and afterwards walk through the park to Bassenthwaite Lake, the wildflower meadow or the Norman church of St Brega.

**Open:** 30th March to 30th October Sunday and Wednesday (also Friday in August) 2.00 to 4.30.

**Admission:** £3.00, child £1.50, family £8.00; grounds £1.00, child 80p.

**Facilities:** Car parking. Home-made food in the tea rooms. Children are especially welcome in the house (where they can take part in quizzes and hunts) and the grounds (there are four adventure playgrounds).

**Disabled Access:** Yes.

**Additional information:** Dogs allowed on a lead.

# DALEMAIN

*Penrith, Cumbria CA11 0HB Tel: (07684) 86450*
*Off A592 (use exit 40 M6)*

**Ownership:** Private

**General Description:** In the middle of the 18th century Edward Hasell added an elegant Georgian façade to what was basically an Elizabethan house. As a result the charming interior gives the impression of having evolved its winding passages, quaint stairways and unexpected rooms, such as the breathtaking Chinese Room with its original hand-painted wallpaper, furniture and fittings. Children, and adults, will be delighted by the Old Nursery with its 'baby house' and the hiding hole in the housekeeper's room. In the cobbled courtyard is a Countryside Museum and, nearby, the 16th-century Great Barn contains the Fell Pony Museum and old agricultural machinery.

**Open:** 25th March to 2nd October, daily except Friday and Saturday, 11.15-5.00.

**Admission:** £4.00, child (5-16) £3.00, Family £11.00; gardens only £3.00, children free.

**Facilities:** Excellent lunches and teas in front of a huge log fire. Gift shop. Car park. Adventure playground.

**Disabled Access:** Facilities for disabled.

**Additional information:** Picnic area. No dogs beyond car park.

# CHATSWORTH

*Bakewell, Derbyshire DE45 1PP Tel: (0246) 582204*
*Off B6012 8m N of Matlock*

**Ownership:** The Duke of Devonshire

**General Description:** The home of the Duke and Duchess of Devonshire is one of the grandest country houses in England. The Elizabethan house built in 1555 by Bess of Hardwick was altered by her great-great grandson William Cavendish, 1st Duke of Devonshire, between 1686 and 1708. The 6th Duke made extensive additions in the 1820s. It is richly furnished and decorated throughout with painted walls and ceilings, elaborate inlay furniture and wall hangings of tapestry and leather. There is a magnificent library and the collection of paintings, drawings, sculptures, silver, porcelain and curiosities is world famous. The remarkable Scots Bedrooms, for which there is an extra charge, can also be viewed.

The Garden covers over 100 acres. It provides many delights and surprises: a cascade, spectacular fountains and rocks, herbaceous borders, rose garden and secluded walks among rare shrubs and forest trees. The surrounding park of 1,000 acres was landscaped by 'Capability' Brown.

**Open:** 23rd March to 30th October every day 11.00-4.30.

**Admission:** £5.50, senior citizens/student £4.75 (Scots Bedrooms £1.00 extra); child £2.75 (Scots Bedrooms 50p extra). Gardens only; £3.00, senior citizens/student £2.50, child £1.50. Family tickets available.

**Facilities:** The Carriage House Self-service restaurant serves home-made food. There is also a farmyard (with daily milking demonstrations) and an Adventure Playground for children. Shops and garden centre. Car park.

**Disabled Access:** Garden only.

**Additional information:** There is a Caravan Club site for 118 touring caravan pitches. Picnics in park or garden. Dogs welcome on leads.

**Special Events:** Angling Fair in May, Country Fair in early September.

*The Emperor Fountain*

# HADDON HALL

*Bakewell, Derbyshire DE45 1LA Tel: (0629) 812855*
*Off A6 Bakewell to Rowsley*

**Ownership:** The Duke of Rutland

**General Description:** England's most complete and authentic medieval and Tudor house set in beautiful countryside with typical English country gardens stepping down to the peaceful River Wye. The house escaped alterations in the 18th and 19th centuries until it was restored to perfect condition at the beginning of this century. The 14th-century Chapel with its fine frescos, the intriguing medieval kitchens and the Great Hall can all be seen as they were 600 years ago. The beautiful 16th-century Long Gallery houses a fine collection of tapestries from the 16th and 17th centuries. The gardens are on six great stone-buttressed terraces which step down to the River Wye. They are filled with scented roses and clematis.

**Open:** 1st April (or Good Friday, whichever is earlier) to 30th September, 11.00-6.00 daily except Monday (and Sunday in July and August). Also open Bank Holiday weekends.

**Admission:** £4.00, senior citizen £3.00, child £2.50.

**Facilities:** Licensed self-service restaurant for coffee, lunches and teas. The gift shop sells Minton 'Haddon Hall' pottery. Car park 50p.

**Disabled Access:** Most of the Hall is not accessible to disabled visitors because of steep steps and different levels.

# HARDWICK HALL

*Doe Lea, Chesterfield S44 5QJ*
*Tel: (0246) 850430*
*6m W of Mansfield; M1 exit 29 & A6175*

**Ownership:** The National Trust.

**General Description:** A late 16th-century 'prodigy house' designed by Robert Smythson for Bess of Hardwick. The house contains outstanding contemporary furniture, tapestries and needlework, many pieces identified in an inventory of 1601; a needlework exhibition is on permanent display. Walled courtyards enclose fine gardens, orchards and a herb garden. The Country Park contains Whiteface Woodland sheep and Longhorn cattle.

**Open:** 30th March to end October, Wednesday, Thursday, Saturday and Sunday and Bank Holiday Mondays 12.30-5.00; Garden daily 12.00-5.30.

**Admission:** £5.50, child £2.70; garden only £2.00.

**Facilities:** Licensed restaurant in the Great Kitchen. Shop. Car park.

**Disabled Access:** Limited access to ground floor via steps to main entrance. Restaurant also accessible via steps. Toilets.

**Additional information:** No picnic facilities. Dogs only in Country Park.

# <u>KEDLESTON HALL</u>

*Derby DE22 5JH Tel: (0332) 842191*
*5m NW of Derby, signs from A38/A52 junction*

**Ownership:** The National Trust.

**General Description:** A Palladian mansion set in a classical park landscape, built 1759-65 for Nathaniel Curzon, 1st Baron Scarsdale, whose family has lived at Kedleston since the 12th century. The house has the most complete and least altered sequence of Robert Adam interiors in England, and the rooms still contain the original great collection of family portraits, old masters, and their furniture and other contents. Indian Museum exhibition of Robert Adam architectural drawings, an Adam bridge and fishing pavilion in the park, and a garden and pleasure grounds.

**Open:** 30th March to end October, Saturday to Wednesday 1.00-5.30. Garden 11.00-6.00.

**Admission:** £4.20, child £2.10.

**Facilities:** Licensed restaurant serving lunches and teas. Shop. Car park.

**Disabled Access:** Difficult steps. Please telephone beforehand. Toilets.

**Additional information:** Dogs only on leads in park. No picnic facilities.

# SUDBURY HALL

*Sudbury, Ashbourne DE6 5HT Tel: (0283) 585305*
*6m E of Uttoxeter at junction of A50/A515*

**Ownership:** The National Trust.

**General Description:** One of the most individual of late
17th-century houses, begun by George Vernon c. 1661. The
rich decoration includes wood carvings by Gibbons and
Pierce, superb plasterwork and mythological decorative
paintings by Laguerre. The Great Staircase is one of the
finest of its kind in an English house.

The National Trust Museum of Childhood is in a service
wing of the Hall with displays about children and childhood.
There is particular emphasis on the Victorian and Edwardian
periods. Betty Cadbury's collection of toys and dolls, from
the 18th century onwards, is displayed in the Toybox Gallery
where there are chimney climbs for *sweep-sized* youngsters.

**Open:** 30th March to 30th September, Wednesday to Sunday
and Bank Holiday Mondays 1.00-5.30. Grounds 12.00-6.00.

**Admission:** £3.20, child £1.60. Joint ticket for Hall and
Museum £4.40.

**Facilities:** Licensed Coach House tearoom serves lunch and
tea. Car park.

**Disabled Access:** Hall difficult. Museum accessible.

**Additional information:** Owing to light levels, visitors
wishing to study the Hall's plasterwork or paintings in detail
should avoid dull days and late afternoons in September.
Dogs in car park only. No picnic facilities.

# POWDERHAM CASTLE

*Kenton, Exeter EX6 8JQ Tel: (0626) 890243*
*Off A379 Exeter to Dawlish*

**Ownership:** Lord and Lady Courtenay

**General Description:** Built between 1390 and 1420 by Sir Philip Courtenay. Surrounded by a deer park the Castle is situated on the west bank of the River Exe estuary. It was damaged during the Civil War but restored and altered during the 18th and 19th centuries. It is still the home of the ancient Courtenay family, Earls of Devon. The Castle contains some fine furniture and paintings as well as very dramatic plasterwork in the Staircase Hall. The Music Room is probably the finest room in the house with Regency furniture, Italian marble and an 18th-century organ by Bryce Seed of Bristol. An elegant terraced rose garden surrounds the east front of the Castle and is the home of Timothy a tortoise who is probably 130 years old.

**Open:** March 30th to 2nd October, every day except Saturday.

**Admission:** £3.95, OAP £3.75, child £2.95, Family £10.95.

**Facilities:** Refreshments are available.

**Disabled Access:** Limited access only.

**Additional information:** Parts of the house were featured in the film, *The Remains of the Day*. Dogs are welcome. There are picnic facilities.

# SHERBORNE CASTLE

*Sherborne, Dorset DT9 3PY Tel: (0935) 813182*
*Off A30 Sherborne to Shaftesbury*

**Ownership:** Private.

**General Description:** This splendid 17th-century house has been the home of two distinguished families. Sir Walter Raleigh started building in 1594. The Digby family moved in in 1617. Inside the rich period interiors there is a priceless collection of paintings (including the famous one of Queen Elizabeth I in procession), rare books, porcelain and family treasures and much variety. The 18th-century Library, for instance, is in a glorious Gothick style whilst the Oak Room has Jacobean wooden panelling. Everywhere there are fine plasterwork ceilings and some huge fireplaces. The house is set beside a large and lovely lake with the ruins of Old Sherborne Castle on its further side. You can take walks around the lake or through the woodlands.

**Open:** From Easter Saturday to end of September, Thursday, Saturday, Sunday and Bank Holiday Mondays from 2.00-5.30. The grounds and tea rooms are open from 12.00.

**Admission:** £3.60, child £1.80, OAP £3.00; Grounds only £1.50, child 80p.

**Facilities:** Ample parking and lakeside tea rooms. Shop.

**Disabled Access:** Very limited access.

**Additional information:** Dogs welcome in grounds on lead. Picnics in the grounds.

# KINGSTON LACY HOUSE

*Wimborne Minster, Dorset BH21 4GA*
*Tel: (0202) 883402*
*B3082 Blandford-Wimborne road*

**Ownership:** The National Trust

**General Description:** A fine 17th-century house, Dorset's grandest. It was designed for Sir Ralph Bankes by Sir Roger Pratt between 1663 and 1665. In 1835 it was altered by Sir Charles Barry. The Library and Saloon are in 18th-century style. The house contains an outstanding collection of paintings including works by Rubens, Titian, Van Dyck and Lely. The 'Spanish Room', fitted out in the 1840s, is in gilded leather with a gilded ceiling brought from the Contarini Palace in Venice. Finally there is an exhibition of Ancient Egyptian paintings and other artefacts brought from Egypt by one of the family. Most of the service buildings for the house are 18th century except for the redbrick stables. The house is set in 250 acres of wooded park which feature an Egyptian obelisk and a sarcophagus of the 14th century BC. There is a replanted Victory Fernery, a cedar avenue, a lime walk and a sunken garden.

**Open:** 26th March to 30th October, daily except Thursday and Friday, 12.00-5.30. Park 11.30-6.00.

**Admission:** £5.20, child £2.60; garden and park £2.00, child £1.00.

**Facilities:** Lunches and teas in Licensed Stable Restaurant. Ample car parking. Gift shop.

**Disabled Access:** Access to garden only. Two special days for visitors in wheelchairs. Wheelchair available. Toilets.

**Additional information:** Fine collection of Ancient Egyptian artefacts. Picnics in the park. Dogs allowed in North Park only, on leads.

*The Drawing Room*

# ⊞ AUDLEY END HOUSE

*Saffron Walden, Essex CB11 4JF Tel: (0799) 522399*
*1m W of Saffron Walden on B1383*

**Ownership:** English Heritage

**General Description:** Glimpsed across the superb landscaped park, Audley End with the columns of its twin porches and the distinctive turquoise caps of its turrets is one of the great sights of East Anglia, a Jacobean palace without equal. The richly decorated interiors are now arranged to show how they would have appeared at particular periods. The Little Drawing Room was designed by Robert Adam; the Great Hall has a massive Jacobean screen and there is a 'Gothick' chapel. Lord Braybrooke's Sitting Room houses the cream of the furniture and pictures (including works by Canaletto and Van Goyen). The park is a pastoral landscape created by 'Capability' Brown with an Elysian Garden, an elegant Robert Adam bridge and a classical Temple of Concord. There is also a Victorian parterre garden designed by William Gilpin in the 1830s.

**Open:** 1st April to 30th September, Wednesday to Sunday (and Bank Holidays) 1.00-6.00. Gardens open at 12.00.

**Admission:** £5.20, Concessions £3.90, child £2.60. Grounds: £2.85, Concessions £2.15, child £1.40.

**Facilities:** Restaurant, gift shop and garden centre. Car park.

**Disabled Access:** Most of the ground floor and gardens are acessible. Toilets.

**Additional information:** Picnic tables.

**Special events:** There are a series of events in the summer.

# SNOWSHILL MANOR

*Nr Broadway, Worcs WR12 7JU Tel: (0386) 852410*
*3m SW of Broadway turning off A44*

**Ownership:** The National Trust

**General Description:** A Tudor house with a façade built around 1700, Snowshill is no ordinary Cotswold manor house but the setting for Charles Wade's collection of craftsmanship. These include English, European and Oriental furniture, musical instruments, craft tools, toys, clocks, weaver's and spinner's tools and bicycles. They are displayed in 21 rooms of the house. The Green Room contains a large number of suits of Japanese Samurai armour arranged to give the impression of a company of warriors meeting in the gloom. Visitors can also see Wade's inventively equipped cottage and the charming garden he created, as a series of old-fashioned cottage gardens.

**Open:** April and October, Saturday and Sunday 1.00-5.00; May to end of September, daily (except Tuesday) 1.00-6.00.

**Admission:** £4.20, family £11.60.

**Facilities:** Car park in village.

**Disabled Access:** There is no access for disabled persons.

**Additional information:** No dogs allowed. No picnics. There is currently no access to the Costume Collection.

# BUCKINGHAM PALACE

*Buckingham Palace Road, London SW1A 1AA*
*Tel: 071-839 1377*
*Green Park, St James or Victoria Tube stations*

**Ownership:** HM The Queen

**General Description:** Buckingham Palace is the official London residence of Her Majesty The Queen and certainly the most famous residence in London. King George III bought the original house from the Duke of Buckingham in 1762 and moved there. King George IV, when he acceded to the throne in 1820, commissioned John Nash to build a state palace and much of today's structure and interior decoration was built then. Nash added to the original rather than rebuilding it. He built the wings at the front and increased the depth at the back. There he created the wonderful Garden Front suite of rooms on the first floor. The building was only completed in Victoria's reign. In 1847 the East Front was constructed by Edward Blore, joining Nash's wings and enclosing the forecourt. Finally the façade was refaced in 1912 to complete the Palace we have today.

The Royal Mews, designed by Nash in the 1820s, house some of the magnificent gilded and polished State Carriages and Coaches together with their horses and equipment. Also nearby is the Queen's Gallery which features works of art from one of the finest collections in the world.

**Open:** State Rooms: 7th August to 2nd October daily, 9.30-5.30; Queen's Gallery: 4th March to 22nd December, Tuesday to Saturday and Bank Holidays 10.00-5.00, Sunday 14.00-5.00; Royal Mews: 29th March to 29th September 12.00-4.00, 5th October to 21st December, 5th January to

23rd March, Wednesday only, 12.00-4.00.

**Admission:** State Rooms: £8.00, over 60s £5.50, under 17s £4.00; Queen's Gallery £3.00, over 60s £2.00, under 17s £1.50, Family £7.50; Royal Mews £3.00, over 60s £2.00, under 17s £1.50, Family £7.50; combined tickets (Mews and Gallery) £5.00, over 60s £3.50, under 17s £2.20, Family £12.00.

**Facilities:** Gift Shop. No toilets.

**Disabled Access:** State Rooms accessible with lift. Please telephone 071-839 1377 ext 4204 for pre-booking service to avoid queuing. Limited parking.

**Additional information:** Large luggage items and cameras not allowed in buildings. No dogs except guide dogs.

# THE BANQUETING HOUSE

*Whitehall, London SW1A 2ER Tel: (071) 930 4179*
*Trafalgar Square, Westminster or Embankment Tube*
*stations*

**Ownership:** Historic Royal Palaces Agency

**General Description:** The present building is all that
remains of the great Palace of Westminster once the
Sovereign's main London residence, destroyed in 1698. It
was designed by Inigo Jones and built in 1622. Charles I
commissioned Rubens to paint the ceiling – the nine huge
canvasses, including two that measured 28 by 20 feet and
two measuring 40 by 10 feet, were eventually put up in 1635.
They are still intact and are a spectacular sight. Later
Charles, on 30th January 1649, was beheaded outside the
north end of the building in Whitehall. Today, however, the
Hall provides an oasis of peace and splendour in Whitehall
although it is still used for magnificent banquets.

**Open:** Monday to Saturday 10.00-5.00.

**Admission:** £2.90, Concessions £2.20, child £1.90.

**Facilities:** NCP car park near Trafalgar Square.

**Disabled Access:** Access to crypt. Toilet.

**Additional information:** Guide dogs only.

# CHISWICK HOUSE

*Burlington Lane, London W4 2RP Tel: 081-995 0508*

**Ownership:** English Heritage.

**General Description:** Chiswick House is internationally renowned as one of the finest English buildings inspired by the architecture of Ancient Rome and Renaissance Italy. Lord Burlington, who built the villa from 1725-9, sought to create here the kind of house and garden that might have been found in the suburbs of ancient Rome, as a fitting setting for his library and art collections. The Blue Room has been specially refurbished for Lord Burlington's tercentenary. Today you can savour the splendour of the magnificent interior decoration by William Kent and the beautiful Italianate gardens, complete with statues, temples, urns and obelisks.

**Open:** April to October 10.00-6.00; November to December, Wednesday to Sunday, 10.00-4.00. Closed daily 1.00-2.00.

**Admission:** £2.30, concessions £1.70, child £1.15.

**Facilities:** No car parking on site but parking on the A4 (westbound). Refreshments available.

**Disabled Access:** Ground floor access only.

**Additional information:** Picnics in the grounds. Only guide dogs.

# HAMPTON COURT PALACE

*East Molesey, Surrey KT8 9AU Tel: 081-781 9500*
*Just off A308; train (from Waterloo), bus and river launch*

**Ownership:** Historic Royal Palaces Agency

**General Description:** The beauty of Wren's building is combined with some of the finest Jacobean architecture in one of the great Royal Palaces of England. From 1525 when Henry VIII first stayed here, the Palace has been a scene of splendour and entertainment. The interiors glow in dazzling reds, blues and greens with gold glinting on the ceilings or elaborate tapestries on the walls. The interiors reflect the many styles and periods of its history. The King's Apartments of William III, restored to their former splendour after the fire of 1986, are peopled with characters from the past and the food they ate. The huge fires are still burning in the Tudor Kitchens although whole animals are not being roasted. There are Henry VIII's State Apartmentts with a spectacular Great Hall, or the Queen's State Apartments built for Queen Mary II in the 17th century. There are Georgian Rooms from the 18th century. In the Wolsey and Renaissance Picture Gallery you can see the great Renaissance paintings from the Royal Collection. Then there is the Haunted Gallery!

In the acres of parkland, apart from the world famous 300-year-old Maze, are Tudor, Baroque and Victorian gardens and the 200-year-old Great Vine planted in 1768 and still flourishing in spite of its twisted stem.

**Open:** Mid-March to mid-October 9.30-6.00 except Monday 10.15-6.00. Mid-October to mid-March 9.30-4.30 except Monday 10.15-4.30. Closed 24th to 26th December. Tudor

Tennis Court and Banqueting House open mid-March to mid-October only.

**Admission:** £7.00, concessions £5.30, child £4.70; gardens free.

**Facilities:** Meals available in the Privy Kitchen, The Tiltyard Restaurant and the Garden Café. Car park.

**Disabled Access:** Lifts for disabled access.

**Additional information:** Picnics in park. No dogs.

**Special events:** Tudor Christmas Festivities, Easter Garden Activites and a Summer programme of special events.

# HAM HOUSE

*Ham, Richmond, Surrey TW10 7RS Tel: 081-940 1950*
*W of A37, S of Thames*

**Ownership:** The National Trust.

**General Description:** An outstanding Stuart house built about 1610 but enlarged, redecorated and furnished by the Duke and Duchess of Lauderdale in the 1670s in the most up-to-date style of the time, much of which survives. The 17th-century garden is in the process of restoration.

**Open:** 30th March to end October Monday to Wednesday 1.00-5.00; Saturday 1.00-5.30; Sunday 11.30-5.30; November to 8th December Saturday and Sunday 1.00-4.00.

**Admission:** £4.00, child £2.00. Garden free.

**Facilities:** Restaurant for lunches and teas. Car park.

**Disabled Access:** Access to house by steep ramps, lift to first floor.

**Additional information:** Picnic facilities in Rose Garden. No dogs allowed.

# KENSINGTON PALACE

*Kensington Gardens, London W8 4PX Tel: 071-937 9561*
*Off Bayswater Road (A40); Queensway Tube station*

**Ownership:** Historic Royal Palaces Agency

**General Description:** The State Apartments reveal 300 years of Court life. The Palace was acquired by William and Mary in 1689 as a country home and part of the building remains a private Royal Residence. The King's Grand Staircase, Queen Mary II's Bedchamber and the Duchess of Kent's Dressing Room evoke the atmosphere of times past. The young Princess Victoria's Bedroom was where she was woken, aged 18, to be told she was Queen. Also open is the Royal Ceremonial Dress Collection, a dazzling display of sumptuous dresses and dashing uniforms, assembled in period settings and showing Court life since the 18th century.

**Open:** April to October Monday to Saturday, 9.00-5.30, Sunday 11.00-5.30. October to March Monday to Saturday 9.00-5.00, Sunday 11.00-5.00.

**Admission:** £4.10, student/senior citizens £3.10, child (5-15) £2.70.

**Facilities:** Tea is served in the Orangery or the Winter Café. No car park. Souvenir shop.

**Disabled Access:** Please telephone in advance.

**Additional information:** Visitor's access is by guided tour only which lasts approximately one hour. No picnics. Guide dogs only.

# KENWOOD

*Hampstead Lane, London NW3 Tel: 081-348 1286*
*210 bus service*

**Ownership:** English Heritage

**General Description:** Standing on the edge of Hampstead Heath, Kenwood is renowned for its important collection of paintings, a Rembrandt *Self Portrait*, Vermeer's *Guitar Player*, Gainsborough's *Countess Howe* and works by Turner and Reynolds. The 18th-century British portraits reflect the tastes of Edward Guinness, 1st Lord Iveagh, who gave his collection to the nation. The house was remodelled in the 1760s by Robert Adam. The Library is one of the finest surviving Adam rooms. The grounds offer a dramatic juxtaposition of 18th-century aristocratic landscaping with the skyline of 20th-century London. Designed by Humphry Repton from 1793, the park with its meadow walks and ornamental lake presents a contrast to the wilder Heath below.

**Open:** 1st April to 31st October, daily 10.00-6.00; 1st November to 31st March, daily 10.00-4.00. Closed Christmas Day.

**Admission:** Free. Donations welcomed.

**Facilities:** Car park.

**Disabled Access:** Access to grounds and ground floor. Toilets.

**Special events:** There are regular summer evening concerts on the sloping banks of the lake.

# KEW PALACE

*Kew Gardens, Richmond, Surrey TW7 3AB*
*Tel: 081-781 9540*
*Kew Road (A307); Kew Gardens Tube Station*

**Ownership:** Historic Royal Palaces Agency

**General Description:** Dating from 1631, Kew Palace is one of the smaller Royal Palaces. George III, Queen Charlotte and their 15 children used it as a family retreat and it gives a rare glimpse of royal domestic life in the early nineteenth century as opposed to the splendour of nearby Hampton Court Palace. Once known as the 'Dutch House' it has great charm and intimacy.
Queen Charlotte's Cottage was a favourite site for royal picnics. Both are set in the world famous Royal Botanic Gardens.

**Open:** April to September: Palace; Monday to Sunday 11.00-5.30; Queen Charlotte's Cottage Saturday, Sunday and Bank Holiday Mondays 11.00-5.30.

**Admission:** Palace and Gardens: £4.30, student/senior citizens £2.60, child (5-15) £2.00; Queen Charlotte's Cottage: 65p, student/senior citizens 45p, child (5-15) 40p.

**Facilities:** The Orangery, Pavilion and Bakery provide food and refreshments. Gift shop. Parking outside garden.

**Disabled Access:** Telephone 081-332 5189 for further information.

**Additional information:** Picnic seats in park. No dogs allowed.

# OSTERLEY PARK

*Jersey Road, Isleworth, Middlesex TW7 4RB*
*Tel: 081-560 3918*
*Via Thornbury Road N side of A4; Osterley Tube station*

**Ownership:** The National Trust

**General Description:** Set in 140 acres of landscaped park with ornamental lakes and woodland walks, Osterley is one of the last great houses still with its original park intact. It was completed in 1575 for Sir Thomas Gresham, founder of the Royal Exchange. Between 1760-1780 it was transformed into a neo-classical villa by Robert Adam for the wealthy London banker Robert Child. The superb interiors contain one of the most complete examples of Robert Adam's work and include plasterwork, carpets and furniture.

Adjacent to the house Gresham's magnificent Stable Block remains largely intact, despite alterations to the doors and windows in later years. Behind lie the Pleasure Grounds with lawns, serpentine gravel paths, beds of evergreen shrubs, a Doric temple and Adam's semi-circular house.

**Open:** 30th March to 30th October Wednesday to Saturday 1.00-5.00; Sunday and Bank Holiday Mondays 11.00-5.00.

**Admission:** £3.50, child £1.75, Family £9.00.

**Facilities:** Parking £1.00. Stables Tea Room serves sandwich lunches and afternoon teas.

**Disabled Access:** Courtesy car from car park. Toilets in park.

**Additional information:** Visitors may picnic in the park. Dogs allowed in park on leads.

**Special events:** Annual Summer Band Concert with Fireworks in Park in August.

*The corner view of the Antechamber Tapestry Room*

# SYON PARK

*Brentford, Middlesex TW8 8JF Tel: 081-560 0881*
*Off London Road (A315) off Chiswick Flyover*

**Ownership:** Duke of Northumberland

**General Description:** This ancient seat of the Dukes of
Northumberland was transformed to the present classical
style by Robert Adam. The sumptuous public rooms are
magnificent examples of Adam's art and include the Great
Hall, nearly a double cube, the richly gilded Ante-Room and
the 136ft Long Gallery. The Print Room has portraits of
many of the people who have made the history of Syon
including ones of the first Duke of Northumberland by
Gainsborough and of the first Duchess by Reynolds. Other
artists represented in the House include Rubens, Lely and
William Kent. There is also a superb collection of furniture
(some by Adam), sculptures and porcelain.
The fifty-five acres of gardens and parkland were designed
by 'Capability' Brown with lawns, meadows and stately
clumps of trees. They were painted by Canaletto. The Great
Conservatory was designed by architect-engineer Charles
Fowler. The world-famous botanical garden was opened to
the public in 1837.

**Open:** April to September Wednesday to Sunday and Bank
Holiday Mondays 11.00-5.00. October Sunday only. Gardens
10.00-6.00 all year.

**Admission:** £4.75, student/OAP/child £3.50; House only
£3.25, Others £2.50; Park only £2.25, Others £1.75;
miniature railway (additional to garden) 75p, child 50p.

**Facilities:** Coffee shop and cafeteria. Shop.

**Disabled Access:** A few steps leading to House but otherwise accessible. Gardens accessible. Toilets.

**Additional information:** There are a great many other features to visit and see on the estate. There is a miniature railway, the London Butterfly House and Garden and Needlecraft Centres.

**Special events:** Monthly antiques fairs; Summer festival in June; Motor Show in June and Craft Show in August.

# THE TOWER OF LONDON

*H.M. Tower of London, London EC3N 4NB*
*Tel: 071-488 5694*
*Tower Hill Tube station; river launch from Westminster*

**Ownership:** Historic Royal Palaces Agency.

**General Description:** 900 years of English history on one incredible site. First and foremost there is a visit to the Crown Jewels in the impressive new Jewel House. The display includes a cinema screen with archive footage of the 1953 Coronation of Queen Elizabeth II and high definitions shots of the major items displayed on larger than life television screens. The White Tower at the centre was built in the 11th century, for defensive reasons, by William the Conqueror and the Tower has grown up about it. Inside the White Tower today there are the Royal Armouries, with their unrivalled displays of suits of armour, artillery and weapons. On the second floor is the superb Norman Chapel of St John. In the basement are the block and axe used for the last execution on Tower Hill in 1747. Many of the other towers are open to the public. The infamous Bloody Tower is where the two young princes in the Tower were last seen alive. Sir Walter Raleigh was imprisoned here for sixteen years. Now there is a reconstruction of his living quarters. On the walls of the Beauchamp Tower are numerous inscriptions made by prisoners over the ages. Along the Wall Walk are the elevated battlements of the inner bailey walls and several other towers. Above Traitor's Gate, under which many a condemned man passed, is Edward I's medieval palace with guides in period costume. Everywhere are the Yeoman Warders of the Tower, the Beefeaters, in their distinctive livery.

**Open:** 1st March to 31st October Monday to Saturday 9.00-6.00, Sunday 10.00-6.00. 1st November to 28th February Monday to Saturday 9.00-5.00, Sunday 10.00-5.00.

**Admission:** £7.95, concessions £5.95, child (5-15) £5.25; family £21.95.

**Facilities:** Gift shops.

**Disabled Access:** There are many difficult and inaccessible areas. Telephone 071-488 5694 for details.

**Additional information:** The recommended minimum time to allow for a visit is two hours. There are no catering facilities within the Tower. Dogs allowed in grounds but not in the towers or buildings.

*Traitor's Gate*

# BEAULIEU PALACE HOUSE

*Brockenhurst, Hants SO42 7ZN Tel: (0590) 612345
B3054 in New Forest, 14m from Southampton*

**Ownership:** Lord Montagu

**General Description:** Although the Motor Museum is the
first port of call on the estate, Beaulieu Palace is still
England's most visited stately home. Once the great
Gatehouse of the Abbey, it has been the family home since
1538. Displays of costumed figures in the House depict
events in the family's history. The Abbey ruins are nearby
with an exhibition of monastic life.

**Open:** Every day (except Christmas Day) April to October
10.00-6.00, November to March 10.00-5.00.

**Admission:** For all facilities £7.50, OAP/student £6.00, child
£5.00, family £23.00.

**Facilities:** Ample parking and restaurants.

**Disabled Access:** Access to most parts of Palace House is
difficult.

**Additional information:** Entry includes the National Motor
Museum, *Wheels*, a ride through 100 years of motoring and a
choice of rides and drives around the estate. Dogs are
allowed in on leads but not in any buildings or on any rides
or drives. There are picnic sites.

# BROADLANDS

*Romsey, Hants SO51 9ZD Tel: (0794) 516878*
*Follow signs from M27 exit 3 or 2*

**Ownership:** Lord Romsey

**General Description:** Lord Mountbatten's former home is an elegant 18th-century Palladian house with a lovely landscaped setting by the River Test created by 'Capability' Brown. In the elegant interior visitors can see fine paintings (including Van Dycks), furniture, porcelain and magnificent sculpture collected by the second Viscount Palmerston, the great Victorian prime minister and a former owner of the house. He wrote in 1736 '... this place all together pleases me above any place I know. Nothing can be more comfortable than this House. It is magnificent when we have company, and when alone it seems to be only a Cottage in a beautiful garden'.

**Open:** 31st March to 25th September, every day (except Friday but open on Friday in August and Good Friday) 12.00-4.00.

**Admission:** £5.00, OAP/student £4.25, child £3.50 (under 12 free); grounds only £3.00, OAP/student £2.00, child £1.00 (under 12 free).

**Facilities:** Tea room facilities. Car park.

**Disabled Access:** Access to most areas. Toilets.

**Additional information:** Audiovisual presentation on Lord Mountbatten and his career as sailor, statesman and military commander. Picnic areas. Dogs allowed in car park only.

**Special events:** During the summer months there is a classic car show, open air theatre, and gardening and craft shows.

# STRATFIELD SAYE HOUSE

*Basingstoke, Hampshire Tel: (0256) 882882*
*Off A33, midway M4 exit 11, M3 exit 6*

**Ownership:** The Duke of Wellington

**General Description:** After Waterloo the Duke of Wellington (or the Great Duke as he was universally known) was
regarded as the saviour of his country and of Europe. A
grateful nation voted a large sum of money to buy him a
house and an estate worthy of a national hero, and in 1817 he
chose Stratfield Saye. The house is still the home of the
present Duke and Duchess of Wellington and retains many of
his personal belongings and much of the atmosphere created
by the Great Duke. The south stable block houses the
Wellington Exhibition which portrays the Great Duke's life
as a soldier and politician. A major feature of this exhibition
is the 18 ton Funeral Hearse constructed from the metal of
French cannons captured at Waterloo and used at the Great
Duke's funeral in 1852.
The gardens include the grave of Copenhagen, the Great
Duke's favourite charger, buried here in 1836.

**Open:** 1st May to 25th September, daily 11.30-4.00 except
Friday.

**Admission:** £4.50, child £2.25.

**Facilities:** Ample parking. Meals served in Stables Tea
Room.

**Disabled Access:** Access to ground floor which is all on one
level.

**Additional information:** Picnic benches. Dogs allowed in
park.

*The Print Room*

# HIGHCLERE CASTLE

*Highclere Park, Highclere, Nr Newbury Tel: (0635) 253210*
*A343 – 4m S of Newbury off A34*

**Ownership:** The Earl of Caernarvon

**General Description:** Designed by Sir Charles Barry, Highclere Castle offers the opportunity to appreciate the special atmosphere of a Grand Victorian Mansion that still retains its air of luxury. Full of treasures, the interior features such extravagant rooms as the Gothic-style Saloon designed by Thomas Allom or the elegant Library with its 7,000 books and Napoleon Bonaparte's desk. There is an exhibition of Egyptian treasures found by Lord Caernarvon who, with Howard Carter, uncovered Tutankhamun's tomb. The grounds include many gardens and the park designed by 'Capability' Brown who planted its famous Cedars of Lebanon.

**Open:** July, August, September, Wednesday, Thursday, Saturday and Sunday, 11.00-6.00 plus Sundays and Mondays of all Bank Holidays except Christmas. Closed July 9th and 10th.

**Admission:** £5.00, OAP £4, child and disabled £3.00. Garden only £3.00.

**Facilities:** Home baked fare in the Castle Housekeeper's Room. Gift Shop. Car park.

**Disabled Access:** Ground floor and gardens only.

**Additional information:** Plant centre. Picnic area. Dogs allowed in car park area only.

**Special events:** These include an Antiques Fair, Flower Show, Concerts, Ballet and Cricket.

# THE VYNE

*Sherborne St John, Basingstoke, Hants RG26 5DX*
*Tel: (0256) 881337*
*4m N of Basingstoke*

**Ownership:** The National Trust

**General Description:** A house of diaper brickwork dating back to the time of Henry VIII. It was built by William, 1st Lord Sandys, in the early 16th century, and extensively altered in mid-17th century, when John Webb added the earliest Classical portico to a country house in England. Within the house there is a fascinating Tudor chapel with Renaissance stained glass, a Palladian staircase and a wealth of old panelling and fine furniture. The house has one of the finest collections of ceramics in the country. Grounds with herbaceous borders and lawns, and lake and woodland walks.

**Open:** 30th March to end September, every day except Monday and Friday (but open for Good Friday and Bank Holiday Mondays when it closes on following Tuesdays), 1.30-5.30 (11.00-5.30 Bank Holiday Mondays).

**Admission:** £4.00; grounds only £2.00

**Facilities:** Tearoom with homemade lunches and teas. Car park. Shop.

**Disabled Access:** Ground floor, tearoom and garden accessible.

**Additional information:** Picnic area. Dogs are allowed in the car park only.

# BERRINGTON HALL

*Nr Leominster, HR6 0DW Tel: (0568) 615721*
*3m N of Leominster, 7m S of Ludlow*

**Ownership:** The National Trust

**General Description:** This elegant, compact house was designed by Henry Holland and built 1778-83 for the Rt Hon Thomas Harley. He prospered as a contractor supplying the British Army in America. His daughter, Anne, married the son of Admiral Lord Rodney. Three of the Admiral's battles are recorded in great canvasses by Thomas Luny.
The interior is richly decorated in the neo-classical taste, the delicate plasterwork frequently inset with painted panels. All the main floor of the house is shown as well as bedrooms, dressing rooms and a nursery upstairs. The Victorian laundry, Georgian Dairy and Servants' Hall (where lunches and teas are served) are in the courtyard, which forms part of Holland's original layout. 'Capability' Brown, Holland's father-in-law, laid out the extensive park in the 1780s.

**Open:** 26th March to end September Wednesday to Sunday (and Bank Holiday Mondays) 1.30-5.30, closes 4.30 in October. 5th November to 18th December, Saturday and Sunday 1.00-4.30.

**Admission:** £3.50, child £1.75, family £9.60; grounds only £1.60.

**Facilities:** Licensed restaurant. Shop.

**Disabled Access:** Access to grounds but limited access to house.

**Additional information:** No picnics. Dogs are not allowed on the property.

# KNEBWORTH HOUSE

*Near Stevenage, Hertfordshire SG3 6PY Tel: (0438) 812661*
*A1(M) exit 7*

**Ownership:** Lord Cobbold

**General Description:** The dramatic skyline of Knebworth House with its turrets, domes and towers, was the Gothic fantasy of Sir Edward Bulwer-Lytton, the Victorian novelist. Behind its exterior the beautiful rooms reflect five centuries of history. The House is an important part of Britain's heritage and is still lived in, and much loved, by the family it was built for in 1490. Many famous visitors have enjoyed its splendour over the years, including Queen Elizabeth I, who stayed here in 1571, and Dickens and Winston Churchill were frequent visitors. The beautiful formal gardens include a Gertrude Jekyll Herb Garden. All surrounded by 250 acres of park with herds of red and sika deer.

**Open:** 26th March to 4th September daily except Monday but including Bank Holiday Mondays 12.00-5.00; gardens 11.5.30.

**Admission:** £4.50, child/OAP £4.00; park and Fort Knebworth £3.00.

**Facilities:** Licensed cafeteria. Ample free parking. Fort Knebworth Adventure Playground.

**Disabled Access:** Limited access only.

**Additional information:** There are picnic facilities. Dogs are allowed in the park on leads.

**Special events:** There is a regular programme of special events, fairs, tournaments and shows.

# HATFIELD HOUSE

*Hatfield, Herts AL9 5NQ Tel: (0707) 262823*
*Close to A1(M); BR trains to Hatfield*

**Ownership:** Marquess of Salisbury

**General Description:** This great Jacobean house, built in 1611, contains famous portraits, rare tapestries, fine furniture and armour and relics of Elizabeth I. There are two exhibitions of special interest – the William IV Kitchen and the National Collection of Model Soldiers with over 3,000 models. Within the gardens stands the Old Palace (1497), childhood home of Elizabeth I. Here in 1558 she learnt that she had become Queen of England. In addition to the 17th-century style formal gardens you can visit the Knot, Scented and Wilderness Gardens or walk along Nature Trails in the Park.

**Open:** 25th March to 9th October, Tuesday to Saturday, 12.00-4.00 (guided tours); Sunday 1.30-5.00 (no guided tours); Bank Holiday Mondays 11.00-5.00 (no guided tours).

**Admission:** £4.70, OAP £3.90, child £3.10. Park, gardens and exhibitions only £2.60, OAP £2.40, child £2.00.

**Facilities:** Restaurant/Coffee shop. Free parking.

**Disabled Access:** Access via ramps and lifts. Toilets.

**Additional information:** Indoor and outdoor picnic areas. Dogs are welcome in park only.

**Special events:** There is a Festival of Gardening in June and a Transport Spectacular in August.

# BURTON AGNES HALL

*Driffield, North Humberside YO25 0ND Tel: (0262) 490324*
*On A166 midway between Driffield and Bridlington*

**Ownership:** Private.

**General Description:** Burton Agnes Hall is a magnificent example of late Elizabethan architecture, lived in by descendants of the original family. The home is filled with treasures accumulated over four centuries, from the magnificent carvings commissioned by the first owners in the Great Hall to the modern French and English paintings of the Impressionist Schools collected in recent years. The garden displays over 2,000 different plants as well as the 'Riddle of the Maze' and giant board games for the young at heart in the Coloured Gardens.

**Open:** 1st April to 31st October daily 11.00-5.00.

**Admission:** £3.00, OAP £2.50, child £2.00; garden only £1.50, OAP £1.25, child 50p.

**Facilities:** Licensed cafeteria. Car park.

**Disabled Access:** Access to grounds and ground floor of house for wheelchairs. Toilets.

**Additional information:** Picnic tables. Dogs welcome on leads in the grounds.

**Special events:** Living History Days, Flower Festival and Gardener's Fair.

# NORMANBY HALL

*Normanby, Scunthorpe, South Humberside, DN15 9HU*
*Tel: (0724) 720588*
*B1430 4m N of Scunthorpe*

**Ownership:** Leased by Scunthorpe Borough Council

**General Description:** The home of the Sheffield Family, formerly Dukes of Buckingham and owners of Buckingham Palace. The present hall was completed in 1830 and is furnished and decorated in Regency style. As well as boasting eight period rooms the recently refurbished Hall also contains costume galleries. The Farming Museum explores country life when farming relied on heavy horses as well as housing the Transport collection and displays of local rural industries. The 350 acres of park include duck ponds.

**Open:** Open daily April to September, 1.00-5.00.

**Admission:** Free.

**Facilities:** Edwardian Cream Teas are served on Sunday in the Hall. There is also a café and gift shop. Children's playground. Car park charge.

**Disabled Access:** Access to ground floor only for wheelchairs. Toilets.

**Additional information:** Picnic area. No dogs allowed.

**Special events:** There are regular exhibitions, rallies, fairs and special days from April to December.

# SEWERBY HALL

*Church Lane, Sewerby. Bridlington, YO15 1EA*
*Tel: (0262) 673769*
*Short drive from town centre or via cliff-top train*

**Ownership:** East Yorkshire Borough Council

**General Description:** An oasis of calm just a stone's throw away from Bridlington's seafront. Established in 1715 by John Graham, the original house stands on the site of a medieval manor and contains an art gallery, archæological displays and the Amy Johnson Exhibition, the pioneer airwoman. The grounds have magnificent gardens, sports and other facilities.

**Open:** Open all year but check by telephone.

**Admission:** Admission £2.00, senior citizens £1.50, child £1.00.

**Facilities:** Clock Tower Tavern and Sewerby Tea Rooms. Free parking. Clifftop railway. Aviaries and Deer Pen.

**Disabled Access:** No access to Hall. Toilets.

**Additional information:** The whole Grounds are full of special facilities such as a zoo, aviary, golf course and children's play area. Picnic areas. Dogs welcome on leads.

**Special events:** There is a full programme of events throughout the year including a Horse Pageant and a Medieval Pageant.

# OSBORNE HOUSE

*East Cowes, Isle of Wight PO32 6JY Tel: (0983) 852484*
*¹/₂m W of Wroxall off B3327*

**Ownership:** English Heritage

**General Description:** 'A place of one's own, quiet and
retired' – this is what Queen Victoria sought and found at
Osborne House. Here, free from court ceremonial, she,
Prince Albert and their family spent many happy years
together.

Commanding panoramic views over the Solent, the house
was designed as an Italianate villa with two tall towers and a
first floor loggia (balcony), all built under the careful
supervision of Prince Albert. It was here that the old Queen
died in 1901, and her apartments have been preserved almost
unaltered ever since. Photographs, paintings, gifts from
visiting dignitaries and mementoes of travels abroad can be
found crowding every room. Amongst Osborne's finest
treasures are the exotic Durbar Room, with its intricate
Indian plaster decoration, and the Horn Room, with furniture
made from deer antlers. On a more intimate scale, the décor,
furniture and paintings in the Nursery bedroom remain just
as they were in the 1870s when Queen Victoria's first
grandchildren came to stay.

Outside on the terrace there are delightful views of the
garden front of the house. The lower terrace contains a triple-
arched alcove in which the royal family often took breakfast.
It was also a favourite spot of Queen Victoria for reading and
writing, and her journal often describes the scent of jasmine,
orange blossoms and roses from the wooden pergola nearby.
In the grounds a Victorian horse and carriage will carry you

to and from the Swiss Cottage, a charming chalet where the Queen's children learnt cooking and gardening. A thatched summerhouse opposite contains the scaled-down implements and barrows used by the children, each painted with its owner's initials. Queen Victoria's famous bathing machine can be seen nearby. Beautifully preserved, Osborne provides a rare glimpse into royal family life in the 19th century.

**Open:** 1st April to 31st October daily 10.00-6.00 (10.00-5.00 in October).

**Admission:** £5.50, concessions £4.10, child £2.75. Grounds only £2.60, concessions £1.95, child £1.30.

**Facilities:** Car parking. Cafeteria close to car park.

**Disabled Access:** Groundfloor only of house. Disabled visitors can be set down at the house entrance. Wheelchairs can be taken on carriage ride.

**Additional information:** Visitors can picnic in the park. No dogs.

*The Drawing Room as it is today*

# CHARTWELL

*Westerham, Kent TN16 1PS Tel: (0732) 866368
2m S of Westerham fork left off B2026*

**Ownership:** The National Trust

**General Description:** Sir Winston Churchill moved with his family to Chartwell in 1924. Except during the Second World War, it was to be his home for forty years. Chartwell is one of the Trust's most popular houses, perhaps because to many people it is nearer to their dream house than grander mansions. The rooms, kept as they were in Churchill's time, evoke the whole of his remarkable career with maps, photographs, books and mementos. There is also a Churchill museum. His old garden studio contains many of his paintings and is open to visitors who can also enjoy magnificent views across the Weald of Kent from the garden.

**Open:** 2nd April to end October, Tuesday, Wednesday and Thursday, 12.00-5.30. Saturday, Sunday and Bank Holiday Mondays, 11.00-5.30. Closed Good Friday and Tuesdays following Bank Holidays.

**Admission:** £4.50, child £2.25; Garden only £2.00, child £1.00; House only (November) £2.50, child £1.25.

**Facilities:** There is a licensed restaurant in the car park. Shop.

**Disabled Access:** House and garden accessible. Lift to first floor. Toilets. Special parking (please telephone).

**Additional information:** Picnic area. Dogs on leads only in grounds. Timed ticket system in operation.

# IGHTHAM MOTE

*Ivy Hatch, Sevenoaks, Kent TN15 0NT Tel: (0732) 810378*
*6m E of Sevenoaks off A25*

**Ownership:** The National Trust

**General Description:** A beautiful, medieval moated manor house with later additions. Special features include the Great Hall, the old Chapel and Crypt c.1340. There is another Chapel with a painted ceiling of c.1520. The newly-restored north-east wing has Victorian furnished rooms whilst the Drawing Room has a Jacobean fireplace, a frieze and an 18th-century Palladian window. An exhibition in the Billiards Room explains the largest conservation programme ever undertaken by the National Trust.

**Open:** April to end October daily except Tuesday and Saturday, weekdays 1.00-5.30, Sunday and Bank Holiday Mondays 11.00-5.30.

**Admission:** £4.00, child £2.00.

**Facilities:** Tea Pavilion. Car park.

**Disabled Access:** Access to ground floor only with special parking.

**Additional information:** Picnic area by car park. No dogs allowed. Timed ticket system in operation.

# KNOLE

*Sevenoaks, Kent TN15 0RP Tel: (0732) 450608*
*S end of Sevenoaks town, just E of A225*

**Ownership:** The National Trust

**General Description:** Knole, the largest private house in the country, was begun in 1456 and greatly extended in 1603 by Thomas Sackville, 1st Earl of Dorset, to whom it was granted by Queen Elizabeth I. It has been the home of the Sackville family ever since. Vita Sackville-West, of literary fame, grew up here. It is said to be a calendar house for it has 365 rooms (one for each day of the year), 52 staircases (one for each week) and 7 courtyards (one for each day). It remains a home and 19 people still live here. The 13 showrooms contain many pictures by famous artists including Reynolds and Gainsborough and magnificent tapestries and one of the most important collections of richly-upholstered 17th-century furniture. The state beds, chairs and stools, including the original Knole Settee, retaining the rich textiles that once sparkled in royal palaces, are now over 300 years old. Everywhere there are old paintings of family members across the centuries. The King's Bedroom, with its resplendent silver furniture and state bed covers in gold and silver brocade, now brings the tour to a triumphant close. Because of the fabrics and other contents light levels at Knole have to be kept low.

**Open:** April to end October, Wednesday, Friday, Saturday, Sunday and Bank Holiday Mondays 11.00-5.00. Thursday 2.00-5.00. Garden open 1st Wednesday in each month, May to September.

**Admission:** £4.00, child £2.00.

**Facilities:** Car park £2.50. Brew House Tearoom.

**Disabled Access:** Access to Great Hall, Park and Garden only. Toilets.

**Additional information:** Warm clothing is recommended in house. Picnics in park. Dogs allowed in park only.

# PENSHURST PLACE

*Penshurst, Tonbridge, Kent TN11 8DG Tel: (0892) 870307*
*From M25 exit 5 on A21; from M26 exit 2a on A21*

**Ownership:** Viscount De L'Isle

**General Description:** The manor house that lies at the heart of Penshurst is the finest and most complete example in England of 14th-century domestic architecture. The great hall, with its vast, sunlit arching chestnut roof and rare octagonal hearth has been described as one of the world's grandest rooms. The 20ft long 15th-century trestle tables it contains are unique. The gardens, too, with origins as old as those of the house are special. They retain their Elizabethan formal framework now seldom found at other great houses, where 18th-century improvers destroyed the ancient structures. Today, the garden rooms, bounded by formal yews, delight with their surprises. They have has been described as the best cared-for formal gardens in England. Penshurst has been the residence of kings and dukes and of the great soldier, courtier and poet, Sir Philip Sidney.

**Open:** March to October every Saturday and Sunday; 26th March to 2nd October daily, 12.00-5.30.

**Admission:** £4.95, concessions £4.50, child £2.75; grounds only £3.50, concessions £3.00, child £2.25.

**Facilities:** The Garden Restaurant serves coffee, lunches and cream teas. Car park.

**Disabled Access:** Access to the State Rooms and the Restaurant is limited.

**Additional information:** No dogs. There are picnic facilities near the car park and in the Adventure Playground.

# LEIGHTON HALL

*Carnforth, Lancashire LA5 9ST Tel: (0524) 734474*
*M6 exit 35 – follow signs*

**Ownership:** R.J.G. Reynolds

**General Description:** The first view of the house is breathtaking. Entering the grounds, the visitor sees the Hall nestling in a hollow at the bottom of the park with the Lakeland Fells rising behind it in the distance. Leighton Hall is the family home of the Gillow furniture-making family and all visitors are treated as guests. The elderly and infirm, for insance, may sit down in the rooms they visit. All rooms are in regular use and there are no ropes or marked-out routes. All tours are guided – often by members of the family. From the old walled garden visitors can take the charming woodland walk, nature trail and a path maze. The gardens won first prize in the North West Tourist Board's Britain in Bloom Competition in 1993.

**Open:** May to September daily except Saturday and Monday 2.00-5.00. August 11.30-5.00.

**Admission:** £3.20, Senior Citizens £2.70, child £2.00.

**Facilities:** Tea rooms for luncheon and afternoon tea. Ample car parking.

**Disabled Access:** Access to ground floor via ramp. Cars can come to the house entrance.

**Additional information:** The birds of prey on view in the aviary area are flown for visitors at 3.30 on open days, weather permitting. Dogs in park on leads. Picnic facilities.

**Special events:** Antiques Fairs, Teddy Bear Extravaganza and Music and Fireworks.

# RUFFORD OLD HALL

*Rufford, Nr Ormskirk L40 1SG Tel: (0704) 821254*
*7m N of Ormskirk on E of A59*

**Ownership:** The National Trust

**General Description:** One of the finest 15th-century buildings in Lancashire. This Tudor Hall, timber framed in late medieval style, is remarkable for its ornate hammer beam roof and screen. Here and in the Carolean wing, altered in 1821, there are fine collections of 17th-century oak furniture and 16th-century arms, armour and tapestries.

**Open:** 2nd April to 31st October, Saturday to Wednesday 1.00-5.00. Gardens 12.00-5.30.

**Admission:** £3.00; garden only £1.60.

**Facilities:** Light lunches (not on Sundays) and teas in licensed restaurant. Shop. Car park.

**Disabled Access:** Access to entrance hall and garden only. Wheelchair available.

**Additional information:** Picnic site near car park. House not suitable for pushchairs or baby backpacks. Dogs in grounds only on leads.

# <u>BELVOIR CASTLE</u>

*Nr Grantham, Lincolnshire Tel: (0476) 870262
Signposted from A1, A607, A52*

**Ownership:** Duke of Rutland

**General Description:** This proud example of early 19th-century architecture stands high above the beautiful Vale of Belvoir, commanding far-reaching views. The castle contains notable collections of armoury, furniture, porcelain, sculpture, silks, tapestries and paintings (including works by Holbein, Poussin, Reynolds and Rubens). All are set in stunning interiors which are a testimony to the craftsmen of their day. The Statue Gardens are terraced into the hillside below the Castle. They take their name from the collection of 17th-century sculptures included within their design. On view today are works from the sculptor Caius Cibber to Charles II. The gardens have been carefully planted so that there is nearly always something in colour. The Duchess's Spring Garden can be seen by pre-booked groups only.

**Open:** 1st April to 29th September, Tuesday, Wednesday, Thursday, Saturday, 11.00-5.00. Sunday, Good Friday and Bank Holiday Mondays 11.00-6.00, Sunday only in October 11.00-5.00.

**Admission:** £4.00, senior citizen £2.75, child £2.50.

**Facilities:** Licensed restaurant serving lunches, coffee and afternoon tea. Gift shop. Car park.

**Disabled Access:** Access limited to ground floor.

**Additional information:** No dogs allowed. Picnic facilities.

**Special events:** These include medieval jousting tournaments held on various Sundays and Bank Holidays.

# STANFORD HALL

*Lutterworth, Leics LE17 6DH Tel: (0788) 860250
M1 exit 19; off A14*

**Ownership:** Lady Braye

**General Description:** The home of the Cave family since 1430. In the 1690s, Sir Roger Cave commissioned the Smiths of Warwick to build the present hall an excellent example of their work and of the William and Mary period. The oldest of the Library's manuscripts dates from 1150. The splendid pink and gold Ballroom has a coved ceiling with four trompe l'oeil shell corners. Throughout the house are portraits of the family and examples of furniture and objets d'art. There is also a collection of Royal Stuart portraits, previously belonging to the last of the male Stuarts. Family costumes are displayed in the Old Dining Room, with early Tudor portraits and a fine Empire chandelier.The Hall is set in an attractive Park. Walled Rose Garden. Stables house Percy Pilcher's replica 1898 Flying Machine..

**Open:** Easter Saturday to the end of September, Saturday, Sunday, Bank Holiday Mondays and following Tuesdays 2.00-6.00.

**Admission:** £3.20, child £1.50; Grounds only £1.80; Motorcycle Museum £1.00, child 30p.

**Facilities:** Home-made afternoon teas in the Tearooms. Free parking. Motorcycle Museum.

**Disabled Access:** All accessible but there are steps to the House and Tearooms. Toilets.

**Additional information:** Picnics beside the River Avon. Dogs welcome in Park on leads.

# BELTON HOUSE

*Grantham NG32 2LS Tel: (0476) 66116*
*3m NE of Grantham on A607*

**Ownership:** The National Trust

**General Description:** The crowning achievement of
Restoration country house architecture, built 1685-88 for Sir
John Brownlow, and altered by James Wyatt in the 1770s.
There are lovely plasterwork ceilings by Edward Goudge and
fine wood carvings of the Grinling Gibbons school. The
rooms contain portraits, furniture, tapestries, oriental
porcelain, family silver gilt and Speaker Cust's silver. In the
grounds there are formal gardens, an orangery and a
magnificent landscaped park with a lakeside walk and the
Bellmount Tower.

**Open:** 30th March to end October, Wednesday to Sunday
and Bank Holidays 1.00-5.30. Garden 11.00-5.30.

**Admission:** £4.30, child £2.10.

**Facilities:** Lunches and teas from the Licensed restaurant.
Shop. Car park.

**Disabled Access:** House difficult – please telephone. Park,
garden, restaurant and shop accessible. Wheelchair available.
Toilets.

**Additional information:** Picnic facilities. Dogs on leads in
parkland only.

# BURGHLEY HOUSE

*Stamford, Lincolnshire PE9 3JY Tel: (0780) 52451*
*1m from A1 at Stamford*

**Ownership:** Private

**General Description:** One of the 'prodigy houses' of
Elizabethan England completed in 1587 – almost golden in
the sunlight. It is characteristic of its time in combining
gothic forms such as the towers and turrets with 'modern'
contemporary ideas from the Continent. There are eighteen
State rooms, including an unusual State Bedroom, which
display furniture, silver, Italian paintings and the Burghley
collection of Oriental and other porcelain. There are fine
painted ceilings by Verrio and Laguerre. 'Capability' Brown
designed the deer park.

**Open:** 1st April to 2nd October daily from 11.00-5.00.

**Admission:** £5.10, OAP £4.80, accompanied child free,
additional child £2.50.

**Facilities:** Orangery Coffee Shop and Restaurant. Car park.

**Disabled Access:** Please telephone for details. Toilets.

**Additional information:** Picnics on the lawn in front of the
house. Dogs in the park on leads only.

**Special events:** The programme includes the Burghley Horse
Trials.

# CROXTETH HALL

*Croxteth Hall Lane, Liverpool L12 0HB Tel: 051 228 5311*
*Off A5058 Ring Road (Queens Drive)*

**Ownership:** City of Liverpool

**General Description:** This great country house in the midst of a modern city reflects the elegance of the Edwardian age when Lord Sefton lived here. A visit can seem like a step back into the past. Upstairs and downstair, character figures show you the everyday life of the family and the servants at work or at leisure. A ground floor display sets the scene, introducing you to Lord Sefton, his family and friends. Other displays cover one thousand years of Molyneux family history with mementos including Lord Sefton's coronet and his carriage. Afterwards you can visit the Home Farm with its traditional breeds in a Victorian farmyard or wander through the Victorian walled garden which includes 'tropical' greenhouses and a mushroom house. The Country Park has 500 acres of woodlands and meadows.

**Open:** Easter to end of September daily 11.00-5.00.

**Admission:** £2.50, child/OAP £1.25.

**Facilities:** Large public car park. Meals and refreshments in the Old Riding School Café. Gift shop.

**Disabled Access:** All accessible except upstairs in the Hall.

**Additional information:** Picnics almost anywhere. Children's adventure playground and miniature railway. No dogs allowed.

# SPEKE HALL

*The Walk, Liverpool L24 1XD Tel: 051-427 7231*
*1m off A561, W side of airport*

**Ownership:** The National Trust

**General Description:** This intricately decorated half-timbered house dates back to Tudor times and keeps its 16th-century hiding places or 'priests' holes' and an eavesdrop chamber. Other, Victorian, interiors have William Morris wallpaper whilst the kitchen and servants' hall reveal the rich diversity of life above and below stairs. The house is built around a cobbled courtyard. The traditional country house garden is being restored in the Victorian style. There is a rose garden, summer border and stream garden. It is surrounded by the ancient Stockton Wood.

**Open:** 26th March to 30th October daily except Monday (but including Bank Holiday Mondays) 1.00-5.30; 5th November to 18th December Saturday and Sunday 1.00-4.30.

**Admission:** £3.40, family £8.50; gardens only £1.00.

**Facilities:** Tearoom serving light lunches and teas. Shop.

**Disabled Access:** Ground floor rooms, garden and woodland walks accessible. Toilets.

**Additional information:** Picnic area in the orchard. No dogs allowed.

# BLICKLING HALL

*Blickling, Norwich NR11 6NF Tel: (0263) 733084*
*N side of B1354 just N of Aylsham on A140*

**Ownership:** The National Trust

**General Description:** Blickling is a spectacular 17th century red brick house flanked by two immense yew hedges. The House contains fine furniture, pictures and tapestries set in magnificent staterooms including the superb Long Gallery with its outstanding Library and spectacular Jacobean plaster ceiling. The Peter the Great Room is dominated by its massive tapestry of Peter the Great at Poltawa. The gardens are renowned for their great yew hedges planted in the 17th century. They also feature a delightful Secret Garden, an 18th century Orangery and a dry moat filled with colourful flowers.

**Open:** 26th March to 30th October Tuesday, Wednesday, Friday, Saturday, Sunday and Bank Holiday Mondays, 1.00-5.00

**Admission:** £4.90, child £2.40; Sundays & Bank Holidays, £5.50, child £2.75.

**Facilities:** Restaurant for morning coffee, lunch and afternoon teas. Shop and Plant Centre. Large car park.

**Disabled Access:** Very good access with a lift to the first floor. Toilets.

**Additional information:** Picnics in the Old Orchard. Dogs only allowed in Park on lead.

**Special events:** Events all year round including Concerts, Fun Day, Rover Car Rally and guided walks.

# HOLKHAM HALL

*Wells-Next-The-Sea, Norfolk NR23 1AB*
*Tel: (0328) 710227*
*Off the A149 coast road Cromer-Hunstanton*

**Ownership:** Viscount Coke

**General Description:** A classic 18th century Palladian-style mansion on the beautiful North Norfolk coast, home to seven generations of the Earls of Leicester. Each part of this majestic house has its appeal, from the stunning grandeur of the alabaster entrance hall, through all the principal rooms filled with art treasures to the old Kitchen, still with its original pots and pans.
In the deer park there are peaceful picnic spots beside the lake and walks to the Temple or the Obelisk down the Ilex avenue.

**Open:** 1st June to end of September daily (except Friday and Saturday) 1.30-5.00; also May, Spring and Summer Bank Holiday Sundays and Mondays 11.30-5.00.

**Admission:** £3.00, child £1.50; Bygones Museum £3.00, child £1.50; Combined ticket £5.00, child £2.50.

**Facilities:** Restaurant, shop and plant centre. Large car park.

**Disabled Access:** Most parts accessible. Toilets.

**Additional information:** Features include Bygones Museum, Pottery and a long stretch of sandy beach. Dogs welcome in park on leads.

*The Marble Hall*

# FELBRIGG HALL

*Norwich NR11 8PR Tel: (0263) 837444*
*2m SW of Cromer off B1436*

**Ownership:** The National Trust

**General Description:** A 17th century house, Felbrigg escaped major alteration during the last 150 years. Now it offers the visitor, as he wanders through the 27 rooms (including the Domestic Wing), a greater understanding of how a country house 'worked'. There are 11 new rooms on display to the public. The Hall contains a superb collection of 18th-century furniture, pictures and thousands of leather-bound books. Out of doors the Walled Garden and Dovehouse are a tranquil area of flower borders and climbing fruit trees from which the visitor can walk to the Great Wood or the lake in the park. Felbrigg houses the national collection of Colchicums (Autumn Crocus).

**Open:** 26th March to 30th October, Monday, Wednesday, Thursday, Saturday and Sunday, 1.00-5.00; Bank Holiday Sunday and Monday, 11.00-5.00.

**Admission:** £4.60; garden only £1.80.

**Facilities:** Park Restaurant and Turret Tearoom for meals. Shop.

**Disabled Access:** Wheelchairs available. Toilets.

**Additional information:** Picnic facilities in park. Dogs on leads in park only.

**Special events:** Felbrigg has a busy schedule of concerts, opera and a Craft Fair.

# OXBURGH HALL

*Oxborough, King's Lynn PE33 9PS Tel: (0366) 328258*
*7m SW of Swaffham at Oxburgh*

**Ownership:** The National Trust

**General Description:** The rooms of this moated house, built in 1482 by the Bedingfeld family show the development of the English house from medieval austerity to Victorian comfort. The main features include the massive Tudor Gatehouse and the views from the roof, a 16th century Priest's Hole and embroidery worked by Mary Queen of Scots during her captivity. The Chapel in the grounds contains a magnificent altarpiece. The grounds feature a 19th century French parterre, a Victorian wilderness garden and a charming woodland walk.

**Open:** 26th March to 30th October Saturday to Wednesday 1.00-5.00; Bank Holiday Monday 11.00-5.00.

**Admission:** £3.80, child £1.90; Estate and Garden only £2.00, child £1.00.

**Facilities:** Licensed restaurant for lunch and afternoon teas. Shop. Car park.

**Disabled Access:** Access to gardens and limited access to house. Toilets.

**Additional information:** No picnic facilities. Dogs in car park only.

# SANDRINGHAM HOUSE

*King's Lynn, Norfolk PE35 6EN Tel: (0553) 772675*
*Off A149 or A148*

**Ownership:** Her Majesty the Queen

**General Description:** The private country retreat of Her Majesty the Queen, Sandringham House is at the heart of the beautiful estate which has been owned by four generations of Monarchs. A grand and imposing building where all the main rooms, used by the Royal Family when in residence, are open to the public. Sandringham House has the warmth and charm of a well-loved family home. Visitors see portraits of The Royal Family, collections of porcelain, jade, quartz, enamelled Russian silver, gold and bronzes set amongst fine furniture.

The sixty acres of glorious grounds that surround the House offer beauty and colour throughout the seasons with a rich variety of flowers, shrubs and magnificent trees, informally planted round lawns and lakes to provide a multitude of tranquil views. In the Country Park there is an adventure playground, tractor and trailer rides and scenic drives. Sandringham Museum contains displays of Royal memorabilia ranging from family photographs to vintage Daimlers.

**Open:** Good Friday to 2nd October daily 11.00-4.45 (opens 12.00 Sunday and Good Friday). The house is closed 19th July to 4th August; the grounds and museum are closed 23rd July to 3rd August.

**Admission:** £3.50, OAP/student £2.50, child £2.00; Grounds and Museum only £2.50, OAP/student £2.00, child £1.50.

**Facilities:** Tearoom, shop and parking in Visitor Centre.

**Disabled Access:** Wheelchair access throughout. Toilets.

**Additional information:** Picnic tables in park. Dogs only in Country Park.

**Special events:** There is a Spring Craft Fair in April, a Spring Spectacular in May, a Country Weekend in June and the Flower Show in July.

*The Small Drawing Room*

# CANONS ASHBY HOUSE

*Daventry, Northants NN11 6SD Tel: (0327) 860044
Either M40 exit 11 or M1 exit 16*

**Ownership:** The National Trust

**General Description:** Home of the Dryden family since the 16th century, this manor house was built c. 1550, added to in the 1590s, and altered in the 1630s and c.1710; it has been largely unaltered since. Within the house, Elizabethan wall paintings and outstanding Jacobean plasterwork are of particular interest. A formal garden includes terraces, walls and gate piers of 1710. There is also a private medieval priory church in the 70-acre park.

**Open:** 30th March to end October, Wednesday to Sunday and Bank Holiday Mondays, 1.00-5.30.

**Admission:** £3.20, child £1.60.

**Facilities:** Light lunches and afternoon teas in Brewhouse. Car park. Shop.

**Disabled Access:** Access to house and garden is by 3 steps. The house is difficult but please telephone for special arrangements. Toilets.

**Additional information:** No picnic facilities. Dogs on leads in Home Paddock only.

# BOUGHTON HOUSE

*Kettering, Northamptonshire NN14 1BJ Tel: (0536) 515731
3m N of Kettering on A43*

**Ownership:** Duke of Buccleuch and Queensberry

**General Description:** Boughton House has been the home
of the Dukes of Buccleuch and Queensberry since 1528. The
500-year-old Tudor monastic building was gradually
enlarged around seven courtyards culminating in the French
style addition of 1695, which has led to Boughton House
being described as 'England's Versailles'. Nonetheless it is a
characteristically English structure of almost village-like
proportions with 7 courtyards, 12 entrances, 52 chimney
stacks and 365 windows. There is an outstanding collection
of fine art including 17th and 18th-century French and
English furniture, tapestries and notable works by El Greco,
Murillo, Caracci and 40 Van Dyck sketches. There is an
incomparable Armoury. All this is set in a 350 acre park with
lakes, parklands and historic avenues of trees.

**Open:** 1st August to 1st September daily 2.00-5.00.
Grounds: 1st May to 30th September daily except Friday
1.00-5.00.

**Admission:** £4.00, OAP/child £2.50 (Staterooms – prior
booking only £1.00); Grounds £1.50, OAP/child 75p.

**Facilities:** Home made fayre at the Stables Restaurant. Gift
Shop. Unlimited parking. Garden centre.

**Disabled Access:** Full disabled access. Free admission to
wheelchair visitors. Toilets.

**Additional information:** Adventure playground for
children. Picnic facilities. Dogs on leads only in grounds.

# LAMPORT HALL

*Northampton, NN6 9HD Tel: (060 128) 272*
*A508 halfway between Northampton/Market Harborough*

**Ownership:** Private

**General Description:** The home of the Isham family for
over four centuries. During the time of the Commonwealth
the Hall was developed from a Tudor manor and is now best
known for its classical frontage started by John Webb in
1655 and completed in the eighteenth century to the design
of Francis Smith of Warwick. In addition to its fine rooms,
including a superb library, the Hall contains a wealth of
furniture, books and paintings collected by the Ishams, many
during the third baronet's Grand Tour in the 1670s. The
gardens include a small Italian garden and a remarkable rock
garden where the first garden gnomes were placed in the late
19th century.

**Open:** Easter to end of September, Sunday and Bank
Holiday Mondays 2.15-5.15; also 2nd, 29th and 30th October
2.15-5.15. Guided tours last two weeks in June 6.30
weekdays, first two weeks in July weekdays at 2.30. Other
Thursday in July and August 2.30.

**Admission:** £3.00, OAP £2.50, child £1.50.

**Facilities:** There is a tearoom and ample parking. Gift shop.

**Disabled Access:** Access to ground floor only.

**Additional information:** Picnic area. Agricultural museum.
Dogs welcome in grounds on leads.

**Special events:** There is a regular programme of music,
theatre, talks and art exhibitions.

# ⊞ BELSAY CASTLE, HALL AND MANOR

*Belsay, Newcastle-upon-Tyne, NE20 0DX*
*Tel: (0661) 881636*
*On A696, 14m NW of Newcastle*

**Ownership:** English Heritage

**General Description:** The Belsay estate encapsulates the history of the Border region from war to peace. The castle, built in the 14th century, is one of the finest examples of a border tower house. Nearby the manor is one of the first unfortified houses to be built in the area. Most extraordinary of all is the Hall. This 19th-century honey-coloured building has the severe elegance and symmetry of a classical Greek temple. Inside the entrance hall is like the central courtyard of a Greco-Roman house. The gardens include the wild and romantic quarry gardens, dramatically planted with evergreens and varieties of exotic plants.

**Open:** 1st April to 31st October daily 10.00-6.00; 1st November to 31st March daily 1.00-4.00.

**Admission:** £2.40, Concessions £1.80, child £1.20.

**Facilities:** Tea room and gift shop. Ample parking.

**Disabled Access:** Full access to gardens and to ground floor of hall.

**Additional information:** Picnic sites. Dogs welcome on leads.

**Special events:** There is a full schedule from May to October. It includes a Vintage Car Rally (August), MG Car Rally (September) plus theatre, Craft Fair and Flower Show.

# CRAGSIDE HOUSE

*Rothbury, Morpeth NE65 7PX Tel: (0669) 20333*
*13m SW of Alnwick (B6341)*

**Ownership:** The National Trust

**General Description:** A Victorian mansion, mainly designed by R. Norman Shaw, in 1000 acres of grounds. It was the first house in the world to be lit by hydro-electricity; the system was developed by the 1st Lord Armstrong with man-made lakes and underground piping. He also planted millions of trees and shrubs and built 40 miles of drives and footpaths. The Power Circuit includes the restored Ram and Power Houses and, in the Visitor Centre, the Armstrong Energy Centre.

**Open:** 1st April to 30th October, daily except Monday but open Bank Holiday Mondays, 1.00-5.30. Grounds 10.30-7.00 also 1st November to 18th December, Tuesday, Saturday & Sunday 10.30-4.00.

**Admission:** £5.50, Grounds and Visitor Centre only £3.40; Family £14.00.

**Facilities:** Morning coffee, lunches and teas. Car park. Shop.

**Disabled Access:** Access to house and most of park.

**Additional information:** Picnicking around Nelly's Moss Lakes. Dogs in grounds only.

# WALLINGTON HOUSE

*Cambo, Morpeth NE61 4AR Tel: (067 074) 283*
*12m W of Morpeth (B6343)*

**Ownership:** The National Trust

**General Description:** Built in 1688 and altered in the 1740s, the house features exceptional plasterwork, fine collections of porcelain, dolls houses, paintings and the Museum of Curiosities. The Central Hall is decorated with paintings by William Bell Scott. The house is set in 100 acres of lawns, lakes and woodland with a beautiful Walled Garden. The conservatory houses fuchsia, heliotrope and bougainvillea.

**Open:** 1st April to 30th October daily except Tuesday, 1.00-5.30; the grounds are open all year round during daylight hours.

**Admission:** £4.40; Walled garden and grounds £2.20.

**Facilities:** Clock Tower Restaurant and shop. Car park.

**Disabled Access:** Access to ground floor and Walled Garden Terrace only. Parts of grounds accessible. Toilets.

**Additional information:** Picnics in grounds. Dogs on leads only in grounds.

**Special events:** Shakespeare at Wallington in June and the Family Fun Day in August.

# NEWSTEAD ABBEY

*Linby, Notts NG15 8GE Tel: (0623) 793447*
*12m N of Nottingham on A60; M1 exit 27*

**Ownership:** Nottingham City Council

**General Description:** Romantic Newstead Abbey is probably best known as the home of the poet Lord Byron (1788-1824) who made it, and its ghostly legends, famous. Visitors to this medieval priory and beautiful historic house are not only able to see Byron's own apartments and an important collection of his manuscripts, letters and first editions, but also the elegant salon and the baronial Great Hall. The gardens with their waterfalls, lakes and ponds are magnificent in all seasons. There are delightful rose, iris, fern, rock and Japanese water gardens to explore.

**Open:** 1st April to 30th September daily 12.00-6.00. Grounds are open all year except last Friday in November from 9.00.

**Admission:** £3.50, Concessions £2.00, child £1.00; grounds only £1.60, concessions £1.00, child £1.00.

**Facilities:** White Lady Restaurant and Coffee Shop. Shop. Car park.

**Disabled Access:** Restricted to parts of the ground floor only.

**Additional information:** Ghost tours on selected dates. Picnic area. Dogs allowed on leads.

**Special events:** The year's special events range from outdoor opera to a Victorian-style Christmas.

# MILTON MANOR

*Milton, Nr Abingdon, Oxon OX14 4EN Tel: (0235) 831287*
*12m S of Oxford; M4 exit 13 and A34*

**Ownership:** Mr Anthony Mockler-Barret

**General Description:** The manor house began its life in 1663 when the present centre part of the house, a red brick square, was built in classical style, possibly to a design of Inigo Jones. In 1764 the wings were added and the interior was extravagantly repanelled producing the 'Strawberry Hill Gothick' Library and Chapel. The house, still very much a family home, contains some fine paintings, furniture and porcelain. The Chapel, which is Roman Catholic, features some superb 13th and 14th-century stained glass and the vestments, chalice and missal of the Catholic Bishop Challoner of London who died in 1791 and was buried here.

**Open:** May to July, Wednesday and Sunday; August, Tuesday, Wednesday, Thursday, Sunday and Bank Holiday Mondays, 2.30 and 3.30 guided tours; gardens 2.00-5.00.

**Admission:** £3.00, child £1.50; Grounds £1.50.

**Facilities:** Refreshments available. Parking area.

**Disabled Access:** Very little access. Ground floor possible. Grounds and tearoom accessible.

**Additional information:** Picnics in parking field. Dogs only in parking field.

# BLENHEIM PALACE

*Woodstock, Oxon OX20 1PX Tel: (0993) 811091*
*8m N of Oxford on A44; M40 exit 9*

**Ownership:** The Duke of Marlborough

**General Description:** The palatial home of the Dukes of
Marlborough and birthplace of Sir Winston Churchill. This
masterpiece of English Baroque was designed by Sir John
Vanbrugh for John Churchill, 1st Duke of Marlborough
during 1705-1722 in recognition of his great victory at the
Battle of Blenheim 1704. The magnificent gilded State
Rooms are full of a fine collection of pictures, sculptures,
antique furniture and tapestries. The Long Library, 183 feet
in length, is of outstanding beauty and houses over 10,000
books as well as a four manual Willis Organ. The many
gardens (such as the Water Terraces, Italian Garden and
Rose Garden) are renowned for their beauty and were
designed, amongst others, by Vanbrugh and Henry Wise.
'Capability' Brown created the park, including the famous
Blenheim lake, in the 1760s. There is an exhibition of
Churchilliana including manuscripts, paintings, personal
belongings , books, photographs and letters. The core of the
exhibition is the room where he was born on 30th November
1874.

**Open:** Mid-March to end of September daily 10.30-5.30.

**Admission:** £6.90, OAP/Children 16 & 17 £4.90, Children
5-15 £3.30. Park and gardens: Cars £3.80, Pedestrian adults
90p, child 50p.

**Facilities:** Licensed restaurant and café. The Pleasure
Gardens include the Maze, putting greens, Butterfly House,

Adventure Playground and Shop. Boats may be hired. Car parking.

**Disabled Access:** Ramps to entrance of house and level tour of house. Access to parts of garden is difficult. Much of park is, however, accessible. Toilets.

**Additional information:** Picnic facilities in park. Dogs in park only on lead.

**Special events:** The Blenheim Audi International Horse Trials in September.

# STONOR

*Henley-on-Thames, Oxfordshire RG9 6HF*
*Tel: (0491) 638587*
*B480 off A4130 N of Henley*

**Ownership:** Lord Camoys

**General Description:** This extended-E shaped building in warm brick is hidden in a fold of the wooded Chiltern hills commanding views of the surrounding deer park. Building at Stonor began around 1280 when the Stonor family had already been living there for over 100 years. Over the next six centuries the house grew. A buttery (now the study), a solar and the Chapel were added between 1280 and 1331. By 1362 an east wing and second large hall had been built. From 1534 Sir Walter joined the building together to create today's E shape. By this time, too, the house had been faced or built in brick. At the Reformation the Stonors remained Catholic. Their medieval Catholic chapel is one of only three used continuously throughout the years of Catholic repression for the mass and is still in use today. It was only in the nineteenth century that the family ceased to suffer financial and social penalties for being Catholic. Today Stonor remains a family home although it contains many items of rare furniture and tapestries. There are paintings by masters such as Kneller and Carracci, drawings by Tintoretto and the Tiepolos. There is an exhibition of the life of St Edmund Campion, the Catholic martyr, who sought sanctuary here in 1581 to illegally print his *Decem Rationes*. The peaceful gardens spread over the hillside with an exhibition of stone sculpture from Zimbabwe.

**Open:** 3rd April to 28th September, Sunday, Wednesday, 2.00-5.30; Bank Holiday Mondays 12.30-5.30; 7th July to 25th August Thursday 2.00-5.30.

**Admission:** £3.50; Chapel and gardens £1.50. Children free.

**Facilities:** Tearoom and gift shop. Car park.

**Disabled Access:** Limited access to house. Ramp access to Gardens, Gift Shop and Tearooms.

**Additional information:** Picnic tables in courtyard. Dogs on leads in grounds only.

*Francis Stonor's Bedroom*

# ATTINGHAM PARK

*Shrewsbury SY4 4TP Tel: (0743) 709203*
*1m NW of Broseley (B4375)*

**Ownership:** The National Trust

**General Description:** This elegant house was designed in 1785 by George Steuart. The classical interiors range from the dramatic red dining room and graceful blue drawing room to the intimate, circular painted boudoir and picture gallery created by Nash with its collection of French and Italian paintings. Fine furniture, an 18th century organ (still played) and Regency silver are also on display. The landscaped park of 250 acres has walks through the deer park and woodland or alongside the river.

**Open:** 26th March to 28th September Saturday to Wednesday 1.30-5.00 (Bank Holiday Mondays 11.00-5.00); October Saturday and Sunday 1.30-5.00. Park open all year, dawn to dusk.

**Admission:** £3.30, Family ticket £8.25; park & grounds only £1.30.

**Facilities:** The licensed tearoom serves home-made lunches and teas. Shop. Ample parking.

**Disabled Access:** Lift to staterooms. Motorised buggy available. Circular Mile Walk is accessible.

**Additional information:** Picnic sites along Mile Walk. Dogs allowed but not in Deer Park.

**Special events:** On many Sundays throughout the year there are conducted tours in the park or rides as well as a Balloon and Kite Fiesta in September with balloon rides.

# WESTON PARK

*Weston under Lizard, Nr Shifnal, Shropshire TF11 8LE*
*Tel: (0952) 76 201*
*off A5, 3m N of M54 exit 3, 7m W of M6 exit 12*

**Ownership:** Weston Park Foundation

**General Description:** An elegant Palladian building designed by Lady Wilbraham in 1671. Today, as well as displaying a fine collection of antique furniture and objets d'art, it houses many paintings including works by Van Dyck, Gainsborough and Lely. The park was landscaped by 'Capability' Brown and the gardens include an Italian Broderie, an Arboretum and the Rose Garden.

**Open:** Please telephone for opening times.

**Admission:** £4.50, OAP £3.50, child £3.00; park and gardens only £3.00, OAP £2.50, child £2.00.

**Facilities:** The Old Stables Tearooms plus licensed bar. Museum of Country Bygones. Car park.

**Disabled Access:** Disabled route – easy access to house. Toilets.

**Additional information:** Picnic facilities. Dogs allowed on leads.

# MONTACUTE HOUSE

*Nr Yeovil, Somerset TA15 6XB Tel: (0935) 823289*
*4m W of Yeovil on S of A3088*

**Ownership:** The National Trust

**General Description:** A magnificent Elizabethan house, with an H-shaped ground plan and many Renaissance features including contemporary plasterwork, chimneypieces and heraldic glass. The house contains fine 17th and 18th century furniture and an exhibition of needlework samplers dating from the 17th century. A large collection of portraits of famous Elizabethan and Jacobean persons from the National Portrait Gallery is displayed in the Long Gallery and adjoining rooms. The formal garden includes mixed borders and old roses. There is also a landscaped park.

**Open:** 26th March to 30th October, daily except Tuesday 12.00-5.30. Closed Good Friday. Garden and park daily except Tuesday 11.30-5.30.

**Admission:** £4.70, child £2.40; gardens and park only £2.60, child £1.20.

**Facilities:** Licensed restaurant for light lunches and teas. Car park. Shop

**Disabled Access:** Access to garden, restaurant and shop only. Toilets.

**Additional information:** Picnic facilities in park. Dogs on leads in park only.

# ❧ THE SHUGBOROUGH ESTATE

*Milford, Nr Stafford ST17 0XB Tel: (0889) 881388*
*Signed from M6; 6m E of Stafford on A513*

**Ownership:** National Trust & Staffordshire County Council.

**General Description:** Originally built in 1693, between 1745 and 1748 the house was extended to feature splendid rococo plasterwork by Vassali, the grounds were landscaped and neo-classical monuments were built. Towards the end of the 18th century further improvements were made by Samuel Wyatt, including the addition of the eight massive Ionic columns that form the grand portico. Fine collections of 18th century ceramics, silver, paintings and French furniture decorate the rooms. There is an exhibition of the photographic work of the present Earl, Patrick Lichfield. In the Servants' Quarters visitors can see the working laundry, kitchens, butler's pantry, brewhouse and the horse drawn vehicles in the coach houses. Park Farm, designed by Samuel Wyatt, features an agricultural museum, rare breeds centre and working corn mill. Costumed guides demonstrate how servants lived and worked over 100 years ago.

**Open:** 26th March to 28th October daily 11.00-5.00.

**Admission:** All sites £7.00, concessions £5.00; House £3.50, concessions £2.00; Park £1.50 per car; Farm £3.50, concessions £2.00; Servants's Quarters £3.00, concessions £2.00.

**Facilities:** Tearoom and licensed restaurant. Car park.

**Disabled Access:** Ground floor of mansion, farm and museum accessible. Toilets.

**Additional information:** Picnic tables. Dogs in the grounds.

# ICKWORTH HOUSE

*Horringer, Bury St Edmunds, Suffolk IP29 5QE*
*Tel: (0284) 735270*
*3m SW of Bury St Edmunds on W side of A143*

**Ownership:** The National Trust

**General Description:** This wonderful Italianate house consists of an immense oval 'Rotunda' with two large wings joined by curving corridors. This ambitious design started in 1795 was the inspiration of the 'eccentric' 4th Earl of Bristol, Bishop of Derry. Today visitors can see fine furniture, the largest private collection of Georgian silver and paintings by Titian and Velasquez. The house also contains an unrivalled series of 18th century family portraits by artists such as Gainsborough and Kauffman. The unusual Italian garden includes an Orangery, hidden glades and a temple rose garden.

**Open:** 26th March to 30th October Tuesday, Wednesday, Friday, Saturday, Sunday and Bank Holiday Mondays 1.30-5.30. Closed on Good Friday.

**Admission:** £4.30, child £2.00; Park and gardens only £1.50, Children 50p.

**Facilities:** Restaurant open for lunches and teas. Shop. Car park.

**Disabled Access:** Ground floor accessible. Toilets.

**Additional information:** Picnic area and Children's play area. Dogs on leads allowed in park only.

**Special events:** Open air opera, concerts and theatre from June to August as well as music in the house.

# CLANDON PARK

*West Clandon, Guildford, Surrey GU4 7RQ*
*Tel: (0372) 453482*
*On A247, 3m E of Guildford*

**Ownership:** The National Trust

**General Description:** Clandon was built in the early 1730s for the 2nd Lord Onslow by the Venetian architect, Giacomo Leoni. This Palladian house with a two-storeyed Marble Hall, contains Onslow family pictures and furniture, the Gubbay collection of porcelain, furniture and needlework, and the Ivo Forde collection of Meissen Italian figures. Also of interest are the old kitchens, the Queen's Royal Surrey Regiment Museum, and the garden with parterre, grotto and Maori House.

**Open:** 1st April to end October, daily except Thursday and Friday (but open Good Friday) 1.30-5.30; Bank Holiday Mondays 11.00-5.30.

**Admission:** £4.00.

**Facilities:** Licensed restaurant for lunches and teas. Car park and shop.

**Disabled Access:** Access limited because of steps in House. Ramp to garden.

**Additional information:** Picnic facilities. Dogs allowed in picnic area and car park only.

# HATCHLANDS PARK

*East Clandon, Guildford, Surrey GU4 7RT*
*Tel: (0483) 222482*
*N of A246 Guildford-Leatherhead road*

**Ownership:** The National Trust

**General Description:** A handsome brick house built in the 1750s by Stiff Leadbetter for Admiral Boscawen, hero of the Battle of Louisburg. The house has splendid interiors by Robert Adam and in 1988 the Cobbe collection of fine keyboard instruments, paintings and furniture was installed and the house was extensively redecorated. The Park was landscaped by Repton and the gardens designed by Gertrude Jekyll. Both have been newly restored and new walks have been opened in the park.

**Open:** 3rd April to end October, Wednesday, Thursday, Sunday and Bank Holiday Mondays (and Friday in August) 2.00-5.30; grounds 12.30-6.00.

**Admission:** £4.00; grounds only £1.00.

**Facilities:** Licensed restaurant for lunches and home-made teas. Car park and Shop.

**Disabled Access:** Access to ground floor, terrace and part of garden only. Wheelchair available. Special car parking and batricar available. Toilets.

**Additional information:** Dogs only on lead in car park. No picnic facilities.

**Special events:** Concerts are held in the House and Park.

# LOSELEY PARK

*Guildford, Surrey GU3 1HS Tel: (0483) 304440*
*On B3000 - follow signs*

**Ownership:** Major J. R. More-Molyneux

**General Description:** This lovely Elizabethan mansion was
built in 1562 by Sir William More from stone brought from
the ruins of Waverley Abbey, now 850 years old. Dignified
and beautiful, the house is set amongst magnificent parkland
scenery and a moat walk. Inside are many fine works of art,
including panelling from Henry VIII's Nonsuch Palace,
period furniture, paintings and wonderful ceilings and
chimney pieces. Queen Elizabeth I, King James I and Queen
Mary all visited Loseley which today is the centre for
producing the famous Loseley dairy products which are
served in the magnificent 17th-century Tithe Barn Restaurant.

**Open:** House: 2nd May to 1st October, Wednesday to
Saturday 2.00-4.00. Also open Bank Holiday Mondays.
Other facilities open on Sunday.

**Admission:** £3.50, child £2.00; grounds £1.50, child 50p.

**Facilities:** The Tithe Barn Restaurant. Car park. Farm Shop.

**Disabled Access:** Ground floor access to house. Toilets.

**Additional information:** There are guided tours of the
Farm, trailer rides and a Nature Trail. Picnic facilities. Dogs
only on leads in car park.

**Special events:** Flower Festival and Craft Fair with a
spectacular Classical Concert with Fireworks in June and a
Classic Car Show in August.

# POLESDEN LACEY

*Nr Dorking, Surrey RH5 6BD Tel: (0372) 458203*
*5m NW of Dorking, 2m S of Great Bookham, off A246*

**Ownership:** The National Trust

**General Description:** Originally an 1820s Regency villa, the house was remodelled after 1906 by the Hon. Mrs Ronald Greville, a well-known Edwardian hostess who held many a party there. Her collection of fine paintings, furniture, porcelain and silver are still displayed in the reception rooms, and there are also photographs from Mrs Greville's albums. Extensive grounds, a walled rose garden, lawns and tree-lined walks provide visitors with further enjoyments. Polesden Lacey has always been a welcoming place; the Queen Mother spent part of her honeymoon here.

**Open:** March Saturday and Sunday only 1.30-4.30; 30th March to end October Wednesday to Sunday 1.30-5.30. Also open Bank Holiday Sundays and Mondays 11.00-5.30; grounds daily all year 11.00-6.00.

**Admission:** £5.50; grounds and garden only £2.50.

**Facilities:** Coffee, lunches and home-made teas in the Licensed Restaurant. Car park. Shop.

**Disabled Access:** Access to all showrooms, restaurant and parts of garden. Self-drive buggy. Toilets.

**Additional information:** Picnic facilities. Dogs allowed in park only.

**Special events:** There is an Open Air Theatre and the Polesden Fair, both in July.

# PETWORTH HOUSE

*Petworth, West Sussex GU28 0AE Tel: (0798) 342207*
*In centre of Petworth (A272/A283)*

**Ownership:** The National Trust

**General Description:** One of the greatest English Country Houses set in a park landscaped by 'Capability' Brown and immortalised by Turner. Petworth was built in the late 17th century. It houses the finest collection of paintings and sculptures in the care of the National Trust. Turner worked here for many years in the early 19th century and many of his pictures are on display. The portraits include Van Dycks and there are carvings by Grinling Gibbons. New features include the reopening of the Square Dining Room and of the old kitchens in the late summer.

**Open:** 1st April to 30th October, daily except Monday & Friday (but open Bank Holidays – closed Tuesday following), 1.00-5.30. Extra rooms open on Tuesday, Wednesday and Thursday.

**Admission:** £4.00, child £2.00.

**Facilities:** Licensed restaurant for lunches and teas. Shop. Car park 800 yds from House.

**Disabled Access:** Most showrooms are accessible.

**Additional information:** Picnics in the park. Dogs on leads in park only.

# PARHAM

*Parham Park, Pulborough, West Sussex RH20 4HS*
*Tel: (0903) 744888*
*On A283 between Pulborough & Storrington*

**Ownership:** Private

**General Description:** A grey stone Elizabethan house whose
foundation stone was laid in 1577. The panelled interior
includes a fine Great Hall and a delightful Long Gallery.
Amongst the contents are an outstanding collection of
Elizabethan and Stuart portraits, many other fine paintings
(by Bellotto and Mytens amongst others) as well as furniture,
Oriental carpets, needlework and objets d'art. In the Great
Chamber the needlework on the great four-poster bed is
traditionally said to have been made by Mary Queen of Scots.
In the Green Room are mementos of Sir Joseph Banks who
sailed with Captain Cook to Australia. The two unique
Stubbs paintings in the room are an impression of a kangaroo
and of a dingo. The flowers in the arrangements in the house
come from the walled garden. In the Pleasure Grounds there
are such delightful features as the Wendy House, a miniature
house built into the walls, other buildings such as the Three
Arch Summerhouse or the balustrade on the Pleasure Pond
and the brick and turf Maze.

**Open:** 3rd April to 2nd October, Wednesday, Thursday,
Sunday and Bank Holiday Monday (also Saturday 16th July),
2.00-6.00. Gardens open at 1.00.

**Admission:** £4.00, OAP £3.50, child £2.00, family £10.00.
Gardens only: £2.50, child £1.00.

**Facilities:** Self-service teas in the Big Kitchen. Car park. Shop and Garden Shop.

**Disabled Access:** Access to house by arrangement. Ramps in gardens.

**Additional information:** Picnics in the garden. Dogs welcome on leads in the gardens.

**Special events:** Parham House Garden weekend in July.

*The Long Gallery*

# THE ROYAL PAVILION

*Brighton, East Sussex BN1 1UE Tel: (0273) 603005*
*Centre of Brighton – A23*

**Ownership:** Brighton Borough Council

**General Description:** 'The most extraordinary palace in Europe', built as a seaside palace by King George IV, the Prince Regent. Home to three monarchs this breathtaking building started as a simple, classical villa by Henry Holland in 1787. It was transformed by John Nash between 1815 and 1822. He decorated the inside in Chinese taste here carried to unique heights of splendour whilst the exterior was made Indian. The thoroughly restored interior now has original furnishings on loan from HM The Queen in these magnificent settings. The extravagant Music Room moved the King to tears when he first saw it. There is the bright blue and pink Long Gallery or the Banqueting Room dominated by its spectacular dragon chandelier and an exhibition of the most important collection of Regency silver gilt on public view. In the Great Kitchen, with its cast iron palm trees, the superb collection of over 500 pieces of copper is displayed. Finally retire to the King's private apartments, along the corridors with real and imitation bamboo furniture and the famous cast-iron staircases. Or there is the simpler loveliness of Queen Victoria's private apartments.

**Open:** Open daily except 25th & 26th December. June to September 10.00-6.00; October to May 10.00-5.00.

**Admission:** £3.75, OAP/student £2.75, child £2.10.

**Facilities:** The Queen Adelaide Tearooms serve light lunches and Regency teas. Pavilion Shop. No private car park.

**Disabled Access:** Wheelchair access to ground floor. Admission free. Specialist tours available for those with special needs.

**Additional information:** Picnics in the public gardens around the Pavilion.

**Special events:** Concerts are held in the Pavilion during the Brighton Festival in May.

*The Banqueting Room*

# ARBURY HALL

*Nuneaton, Warwickshire CV10 7PT Tel: (0203) 382804*
*Off B4102 from Nuneaton*

**Ownership:** Viscount Daventry

**General Description:** Originally Elizabethan the house was Gothicised by Sir Roger Newdegate during the 18th century. The architecture is unique with soaring fan vaults, plunging pendants and filigree tracery all giving such rooms as the Dining Room and Saloon a breathtaking beauty. There is a fine collection of furniture, glass and china. George Eliot, author of *Middlemarch*, was born on the estate and describes it in *Mr Gilfil's Love Story*. The Dining Room was 'like a cathedral ... richly carved pendants, all of creamy white relieved here and there by touches of gold'. The Saloon is like the Dining Room but 'more elaborate in its tracery, which is like petrified lace'. The 17th-century stables have a fine central doorway designed by Sir Christopher Wren. The house is surrounded by lovely gardens and lakes.

**Open:** Easter Sunday to end of September, Sunday and Bank Holiday Mondays 2.00-5.30. Gardens also open on all Monday.

**Admission:** £3.00, child £1.60. Gardens: £1.60, child 80p.

**Facilities:** Home baked teas in the Stables tearooms. Car park. Gift Shop in the Old Dairy.

**Disabled Access:** Limited access. Ground floor of house only. Parts of garden inaccessible because of gravel paths. No disabled toilet.

**Additional information:** The Stables also house the Pinkerton Collection of veteran bicycles. Picnics near car park. Dogs in gardens only on leads.

**Special events:** These include the Arbury Motor Transport Spectacular in June and Rainbow Craft Fairs in June and September.

*The Dining Room*

# BADDESLEY CLINTON

*Rising Lane, Lapworth, Knowle, Solihull B93 0DQ*
*Tel: (0564) 783294*
*W of A4141 Warwick-Birmingham road*

**Ownership:** The National Trust

**General Description:** This medieval moated house dates from the 14th century. It has been little changed since 1633 when Henry Ferrer 'the Antiquary' died. He was squire for almost seventy years and introduced over a long period most of the panelling and chimney pieces. He inaugurated the tradition in Baddesley of armorial glass which has continued until the present day. Hiding places created in the 1590s for the concealment of Catholic priests are shown. The pictures painted by Rebecca Dulcibella Orpen, wife of Marmion Ferrers, remain to show how the romantic character of Baddesley was enjoyed in the late 19th century. There is also a Chapel, garden ponds and a lake walk.

**Open:** 2nd March to end September, Wednesday to Sunday and Bank Holiday Mondays, 2.00-6.00 (grounds open 12.30); October Wednesday to Sunday 12.30-4.30; March Wednesday to Sunday 2.00-6.00.

**Admission:** £4.00, family £11.00; grounds only £2.00.

**Facilities:** Licensed restaurant for lunches and teas. Car park. Shop.

**Disabled Access:** Access to ground floor and most of garden, restaurant and shop. Wheelchairs available. Toilets.

**Additional information:** No picnic facilities. No dogs.

# CHARLECOTE PARK

*Warwick CV35 9ER Tel: (0789) 470277*
*N side of B4086, 5m E of Stratford, 6m S of Warwick*

**Ownership:** The National Trust

**General Description:** The home of the Lucy family since 1247. The present house was built in the 1550s and later visited by Queen Elizabeth I. Rich Victorian 'romantic' interiors were created from the 1820s onwards, and contain important objects from William Beckford's famously extravagant Fonthill Abbey. The River Avon flows through the park, landscaped by 'Capability' Brown, which supports herds of red and fallow deer, reputedly poached by Shakespeare, and a flock of Jacob sheep, introduced in 1756.

**Open:** April to end October, Friday to Tuesday, 11.00-6.00 (closed Good Friday). House closed 1.00-2.00.

**Admission:** £4.00, family £11.00.

**Facilities:** Orangery Restaurant open for meals. Car park. Gift shop.

**Disabled Access:** Access to all rooms except Gatehouse Museum. Wheelchairs available. Visitors can be dropped off near house. Toilets.

**Additional information:** Picnics allowed in deer park. Dogs in car park on leads only.

**Special events:** Midsummer Music Festival.

# PACKWOOD HOUSE

*Lapworth, Solihull B94 6AT Tel: (0564) 782024*
*On A3400 2m E of Hockley Heath*

**Ownership:** The National Trust

**General Description:** This magnificent timber-framed Tudor house is surrounded by gardens and parkland, with pleasant views from the lakeside walk. The house itself contains a connoisseur's collection of fine textiles, rich tapestries with panelling and furniture to reflect the spirit of the age. The gardens are noted for their formal Carolean Garden as well as the famous yew garden whose topiary is said to represent the Sermon on the Mount.

**Open:** April to end September, Wednesday to Sunday and Bank Holiday Mondays 2.00-6.00 (closed Good Friday); October Wednesday to Sunday 12.30-4.30.

**Admission:** £3.20, Family £8.80; garden only £2.00

**Facilities:** Car park. No refreshments.

**Disabled Access:** Access to ground floor and parts of garden.

**Additional information:** Picnic facilities opposite main gates. No dogs.

# RAGLEY HALL

*Alcester, Warwickshire B49 5NJ Tel: (0789) 762090*
*M42 exit 3 (A435)/M40 exit 15 (A46)*

**Ownership:** Earl of Yarmouth

**General Description:** This Palladian building, housing a superb collection of furniture, paintings and china, was built in 1680. The Great Hall is a magnificent centrepiece to the House, decorated with England's finest baroque plasterwork designed by Gibb. The South Staircase, equally stunning, has the modern mural 'The Temptation' by Graham Rust. Ragley Hall is the Warwickshire home of the Earl and Countess of Yarmouth and has been the seat of the Conway-Seymour family since it was built in 1680. It is set in 400 acres of parkland and garden, which includes the Maze and woodland walks.

**Open:** 2nd April to 2nd October, Tuesday, Wednesday, Thursday, Saturday and Sunday, 1.00-5.00 (Grounds 10.00-6.00).

**Admission:** £5.00, OAP £4.00, child £3.50; garden and park only adults/OAP £4.00, child £2.50.

**Facilities:** Tearoom in house. Car park.

**Disabled Access:** Lift and toilets for house.

**Additional information:** Picnic area. Dogs on leads in park only.

**Special events:** Outdoor concerts in August and September, Game Fair in August and Transport Show in July.

# BOWOOD HOUSE

*Calne, Wiltshire SN11 0LZ Tel: (0249) 812102*
*Off A4 in Derry Hill village*

**Ownership:** Earl and Countess of Shelburne

**General Description:** The House, a wonderful example of Georgian architecture designed by Robert Adam, is what is left of a much bigger establishment which was demolished in 1955. On the ground floor is a magnificent Library of 5,000 volumes, a Laboratory in which Dr Joseph Priestly discovered oxygen in 1774 and the Orangery which was converted into a picture gallery by the present Earl's father. There is also a family Chapel and Sculpture Gallery. Amongst the contents are Victoriana, Indiana, silver, porcelain and paintings including drawings by Bonington and watercolours by Turner. The lovely park, extending over 90 acres, was designed by 'Capability' Brown in the 1760s and there are also magnificent Rhododendron Walks. The grounds themselves have some fine buildings including the Mausoleum built to Adam's design in 1761 and the Doric Temple. There is a superb cascade designed by Hamilton at one end of the lake.

**Open:** 26th March to 30th October daily 11.00-5.30.

**Admission:** £4.50, OAP £4.00, child £2.30.

**Facilities:** Licensed Restaurant, Garden Tearoom and Sandwich Box. Large car park. Adventure playground.

**Disabled Access:** Ground floor of house only. Toilets.

**Additional information:** Picnic facilities. No dogs.

# LONGLEAT HOUSE

*Longleat, Warminster, Wilts BA12 7NW Tel: (0985) 844400*
*Off A350 nr Warminster*

**Ownership:** Marquess of Bath

**General Description:** An architectural masterpiece, one of
the most perfectly classical Elizabethan mansions, designed
by its original owner Sir John Thynne in the 16th century. It
is crammed with priceless paintings, antiques of various
kinds and the finest private library in the world, as well as
some unusual family mementos. The grounds were landscaped by 'Capability' Brown between 1757 and 1762. The
site has numerous other attractions including the Safari Park,
Butterfly Garden, the Marquess of Bath's paintings, the
world's largest maze and the Bygones 'Time Capsule'.

**Open:** Daily 10.00-6.00 Easter to 31st October, 10.00-4.00
rest of year. The Safari Park is open from 12th March to 31st
October from 10.00-6.00.

**Admission:** All attractions £10.00, child 8.00; Safari Park
only £5.50, child £3.50.

**Facilities:** Restaurants, pub and shops. Car park.

**Disabled Access:** Please telephone for information.

**Additional information:** Caravan site for 150 pitches. Dogs
on leads in restricted areas.

# WILTON HOUSE

*Wilton, Salisbury, Wiltshire SP2 0BJ Tel: (0722) 743115*
*A30 3m W of Salisbury in Wilton*

**Ownership:** Earl of Pembroke

**General Description:** Inigo Jones incorporated one original Tudor tower in his 17th century, Palladian-style design alongside magnificent State Rooms which include the famous 'Double Cube'. Morris' Palladian Bridge (1737) and Wyatt's Victorian Gothick cloisters complete the main architectural features visible today. With some 230 original works of art on show, including Van Dyck, Reynolds, Rembrandt, Lely and Brueghel, Wilton House boasts what is reputedly one of Britain's finest private collections.
Visitors are introduced to its history through a dynamic film, narrated by and featuring Anna Massey. Taking the part of one of the early nuns from the original convent on the site, she brings to life, with the help of other professional actors, key episodes in the life of the family and the estate, including the Black Death, a homicidal, drunken Earl and its use as Southern Command HQ in 1943/44. After the House visitors will also see the 18th-century Riding School, the Tudor Kitchen, Dolls House exhibition and much more.
Outside there are 21 acres of landscaped parkland and gardens with quiet woodland and riverside walks, rose and water gardens and a children's adventure playground.

**Open:** 29th March to 30 October, daily 11.00-6.00.

**Admission:** £5.50, OAP £4.50, child £3.50. Family ticket £14.50.

**Facilities:** Fully licensed self-service restaurant. Gift shop.

Large car park.

**Disabled Access:** Full wheelchair access to all areas.

**Additional information:** Picnic facilities. No dogs.

*The Single Cube Room*

# BENINGBROUGH HALL

*Shipton-by-Beningborough, York YO6 1DD*
*Tel: (0904) 470666*
*8m NW of York on A19*

**Ownership:** The National Trust

**General Description:** A striking redbrick Georgian country house, set in magnificent parkland, built by John Bourchier in 1716. The house contains unique wood carvings, an impressive cantilevered staircase, furniture, porcelain and over 100 portraits on loan from the National Portrait Gallery. There is a servants exhibition, a well-equipped Victorian laundry and a 7-acre garden.

**Open:** 30th March to 30th October, Monday, Tuesday, Wednesday, Saturday, Sunday and Good Friday. Also Friday in July and August, 11.00-5.00.

**Admission:** £4.50, child £2.30 (children free during school holidays); Garden and exhibition only £3.00, child £1.50.

**Facilities:** Homemade lunches and teas in the Tearoom. Car Park. Shop. Wilderness play area for children. Visitors may play croquet – equipment is for hire.

**Disabled Access:** Access to ground floor and most facilities. Toilets.

**Additional information:** There are regularly changing exhibitions in the Stable block. Picnic area. No dogs.

# BRAMHAM PARK

*Wetherby, West Yorkshire LS23 6ND Tel: (0937) 844265*
*W of A1 5m S of Weatherby*

**Ownership:** George Lane Fox

**General Description:** A splendid Queen Anne mansion restored in 1906 after a disastrous fire. The house contains a fine collection of furniture, porcelain and paintings including portraits by Kneller and Reynolds. It is set in 66 acres of formal gardens, unique in Britain for their 'grand vista' design inspire by André le Notre, who created Versailles. They remain as they were originally laid out over 250 years ago with ponds, cascades, hedges and loggias. Three long vistas stretch into the pleasure grounds of Black Fen where the more natural and wilder habitat provide a wilder counterpoint to this formalism with nature trails radiating from temples and an Obelisk. The old kitchens are now a museum and photograph gallery. A huge log fire often burns in the great kitchen fireplace.

**Open:** 19th June to 4th September, Sunday, Tuesday, Wednesday and Thursday, 1.15-5.30. Gardens also open for three spring Bank Holiday Sundays and Mondays.

**Admission:** £3.00, OAP £2.00, child £1.00; Grounds only, £2.00, OAP £1.50, child 50p.

**Facilities:** Car park. There are no catering facilities.

**Disabled Access:** Access to gardens only.

**Additional information:** Picnics on seats in garden. Dogs welcome on leads in garden.

# DUNCOMBE PARK

*Helmsley, York YO6 5EB Tel: (0439) 770213*
*Centre of Helmsley*

**Ownership:** Lord & Lady Feversham

**General Description:** Only open to the public since 1991 Duncombe Park has, since 1985, been extensively restored employing the finest British craftsmen. Built in 1713 the house was largely rebuilt after a fire in 1879. The principal rooms are a fine example of the 'grand interior' popular in the late 19th century. The family pictures and collection of English and Continental furniture are on show. The unique, early 18th-century 'green' garden uses the natural landscape to create a tranquil setting for leisurely walks.

**Open:** 1st to 5th April every day; Wednesday and Sunday only in rest of April and October; May to June & September (closed 15th to 16th June) daily except Friday and Saturday; July and August daily: 11.00-4.30.

**Admission:** £4.50, OAP/student £3.75, child (10-16) £2.00. Garden and Park £2.75, child £1.00; Park £1.00.

**Facilities:** Licensed Restaurant and Coffee Shop. Car Park.

**Disabled Access:** Very limited due to gravel paths and steep slopes.

**Additional information:** Picnic facilities. Year round demonstrations of crafts, music, cooking etc. Dogs in park on leads.

**Special events:** The wide programme includes re-enacted battles, a Steam Rally and concerts.

# EAST RIDDLESDEN HALL

*Bradford Road, Keighley BD20 5EL Tel: (0535) 607075*
*1m NE of Keighley on S side of Bradford Road*

**Ownership:** The National Trust

**General Description:** Built at the time of the Civil War by James Murgatroyd, a passionate Royalist. This delightful merchant's house provides a fine setting for its collection of embroidery, pewter and Yorkshire oak furniture. It also features one of the North's greatest barns filled with a collection of traditional agricultural machinery. The tranquil walled garden has been restored to its original formal design. Medieval, monastic fishponds (with ducks) in the grounds run down to the River Aire. Finally, a grass maze and lots of ghosts complete what you will find.

**Open:** 26th March to 30th October, Saturday to Wednesday and Good Friday (also Thursday in July and August), 1.00-5.00.

**Admission:** £3.00, child £1.50 (children free during school holidays).

**Facilities:** Delicious lunches and teas in the tearoom in the old Bothy. Also a gift shop. Car park.

**Disabled Access:** Only upper floor of house inaccessible.

**Additional information:** Picnic facilities. Dogs on leads in grounds.

**Special events:** Full programme includes Elizabethan Revels in July, Circus Skills and Spills, Family Fun Day, a Charleston Party and a Halloween Happening.

# FAIRFAX HOUSE

*The Dining Room*

*Castlegate, York YO1 1RN Tel: (0904) 655543*
*Centre of York close to Cliffords Tower*

**Ownership:** York Civic Trust

**General Description:** This classic 18th-century townhouse has superbly decorated plasterwork, wood and wrought iron lovingly restored. It also houses the Noel Terry Collection of 18th-century furniture and clocks (described by Christies as the finest this century) which give a 'lived-in' feel.

**Open:** 1st March to 31st December every day except Friday.

**Admission:** £3.00, OAP/student £2.50, child £1.50.

**Disabled Access:** With the help of staff. Please telephone.

**Additional information:** No dogs. Small terrace for picnics.

# LOTHERTON HALL

*Leeds LS25 3EB Tel: (0532) 813259*
*1m E of A1 at Aberford on B1217 Towton Road*

**Ownership:** City of Leeds

**General Description:** The charming Edwardian home of the Gascoigne family now contains the Gascoigne art collection including family portraits, opulent race cups, furniture, contemporary crafts, fashion galleries, an Oriental Gallery (Chinese ceramics from the neolithic period to the beginning of the Ming dynasty) and other works of art. The gardens are being replanted with old varieties to recreate Gwendolen Gascoigne's Edwardian garden. There is also a Bird Garden (separate admission) and park.

**Open:** Daily Tuesday to Sunday and Bank Holiday Mondays, 10.30-5.30. Closed 12.00-1.00 October to March.

**Admission:** £2.00, concessions £1.00, child 50p.

**Facilities:** Light meals and teas from the Stables Café (as well as a kiosk). Shop. Ample car parking.

**Additional information:** There is a video film which offers a good introduction to the house and the Gascoigne family. Picnics in the park.

# HAREWOOD HOUSE

*Harewood, Leeds LS17 9LQ Tel: (0532) 886331*
*7m from Leeds and Harrogate on A61*

**Ownership:** Lord Harewood

**General Description:** Harewood House, the Lascelles family home for over 200 years, is an architectural master-piece. Designed by John Carr of York and built over thirteen years between 1759 and 1772, its spectacular interior boasts exquisite plasterwork ceilings by Joseph Rose to designs by Robert Adam decorated by Angelica Kaufman, Biagio Rebecca and Antonio Zucchi. It contains unrivalled 18th-century English furniture made especially for particular rooms in Harewood by Thomas Chippendale. The paintings in the collection include family portraits by Reynolds, Gainsborough, Romney, Hoppner and Lawrence, landscapes by Turner and Girtin, and Renaissance masterpieces by Bellini, El Greco, Tintoretto, Titian and Veronese. A remarkable collection of fine Chinese porcelain and Sèvres and Crown Derby china completes this wonderful array. The house is surrounded by 1000 acres of parkland, gardens and woodland shaped by 'Capability' Brown.

**Open:** 13th March to 31st October, daily 11.00-5.00; grounds 10.00-7.00.

**Admission:** £5.75, OAP £5.00, child/student £3.00, Family £16.00; Bird Garden and grounds £4.50, OAP £2.50, child £2.50, Family £12.00; Terrace Gallery and Grounds £4.50, OAP £1.00, child £1.00.

**Facilities:** The Courtyard Cafés offer a full range of meals. Ample parking. Boat trips. The Terrace Gallery - exhibitions.

**Disabled Access:** Full access to House. Parts of garden difficult.

**Additional information:** Dogs welcome outside of house. Picnics in the park.

**Special events:** The busy schedule of events at Harewood includes Gallery concerts in the Long Gallery, Rallies – Steam, BMW, MG, Rolls Royce, Jaguar – and Festivals for Country and Western Music and Crafts. In addition there are a series of Open Air Concerts.

*The Library*

# CASTLE HOWARD

*York YO6 7DA Tel: (0653) 648444*
*15m N of York off the A64*

**Ownership:** Hon Simon Howard

**General Description:** Magnificent in its scale, splendid in
its opulence and breathtaking in its beauty – Castle Howard
is all of these and more. This 18th century palace, the setting
for TV series *Brideshead Revisited*, is an outstanding
example of Sir John Vanbrugh's art that has always been
open to the public. There are superb public rooms and
galleries – the Great Hall, the Castle Howard Bedroom, Lady
Georgiana's Bedroom and Dressing Room, the Antique
Passage, the Music Room, the Tapestry Room, the Museum
Room, the Long Gallery and the Chapel. All are richly
furnished and filled with such family treasures as pictures,
statues and fine furniture.

Surrounding and dominated by the House are over 1,000
acres of parkland with lawns, woods, nature walks, scenic
lake, the lovely Atlas fountain (which featured so promi-
nently in the television series) and the Temple of the Four
Winds.

**Open:** 18th March to 31st October daily 11.00-4.30 (grounds
open 10.00).

**Admission:** £6.00, OAP £5.00, child £3.00.

**Facilities:** A self-service cafeteria and Lakeside Café are
open in the High Season. Large car park. Boat trips on lake
and tractor-train rides through the park. Adventure Playground. Plant centre.

**Disabled Access:** House (except Chapel) accessible using chairlift.

**Additional information:** Picnicking anywhere in the grounds. Dogs on leads in grounds only.

# <u>NEWBY HALL</u>

*Ripon, North Yorkshire HG4 5AE*
*Tel: (0423) 322583*
*2m from A1 signed/4m from Ripon off B6265 signed*

**Ownership:** Mr & Mrs Robin Compton

**General Description:** Newby Hall is one of the finest Robert Adam houses and provides very beautiful examples of 18th-century interior decoration. It has recently been restored to its original beauty. The superb rooms include the exquisite Gobelins Tapestry Room lined with these rare and subtle works of art. In the glorious Sculpture Gallery works of classical statuary are displayed beneath a vaulting rotunda which fills the room with light. The walls of the Print Bedroom are lined with charming prints. And on display everywhere is some of Chippendale's finest furniture.
The 25 acres of garden are full of rare and beautiful plants – in the clash of colour in the Wars of the Roses Garden, the peace of Sylvia's Garden or the water or rock gardens. The National Collection of Cornus is held at Newby.

**Open:** 1st April to 30th September, Tuesday to Sunday and Bank Holiday Mondays, 12.00-5.00; gardens open earlier at 11.00.

**Admission:** £5.20, OAP £4.00; child £3.00; gardens £3.30, OAP £2.60, child £2.20.

**Facilities:** Licensed Garden restaurant. Car park. For children there is a miniature steam railway through the grounds and an exciting Adventure Garden whose special features include its own river and boats with a bridge going over them. There is also a shop and Plant Stall.

**Disabled Access:** All accessible using ramps. There are wheelchairs for loan. Toilets.

**Additional information:** Another attraction is the Woodland Discovery Walk through the grounds. Picnic area. No dogs except in picnic area.

**Special events:** There are Rainbow Craft Fairs on 11-12th June and 17-18th September and the Northern Country Fair on 19th June. There is a rally for the North East Club for Pre-War Austins on 17th July.

# NOSTELL PRIORY

*Doncaster Road, Wakefield, West Yorkshire WF4 0TH*
*Tel: (0924) 863892*
*On A638 Wakefield-Doncaster road*

**Ownership:** The National Trust (managed by Lord St Oswald)

**General Description:** A fine Palladian house, built for the Winn family in 1733. An additional wing and many of the state rooms were designed by Adam. The Priory houses one of England's finest collections of Chippendale furniture, which was specially made for the house. There are lakeside walks through the grounds.

**Open:** Weekends only March to July. Then every day except Friday July to September 8th. Then weekends only to end of October. Bank Holiday Mondays and Tuesdays. 12.00-5.00 (Sundays and Bank Holidays 11.00-5.00).

**Admission:** £3.50, child £1.80; grounds only £2.20, child £1.10.

**Facilities:** Light lunches and teas available in the Stable Block. Car park. 2 Gift Shops.

**Disabled Access:** All floors accessible (lift). Disabled visitors may usually be driven to the front door. Grounds accessible. Wheelchairs and batricar available.

**Additional information:** Guided tours only at weekends. Picnic facilities. Dogs on leads allowed in grounds only.

# NUNNINGTON HALL

*Nunnington, York YO6 5UY Tel: (0439) 748283*
*In Ryedale 4m SE of Helmsley (A170)*

**Ownership:** The National Trust

**General Description:** Sheltered in a walled garden beside a quiet riverbank, this delightful manor house has remained a much loved home for over 400 years. A magnificent oak panelled hall with a fine carved chimneypiece leads to cosy family living rooms, the nursery and the maids' room. There are panelled bedrooms, fine tapestries and china. You can explore the attics and discover the Carlisle Collection of miniature rooms, one eighth life size, fully furnished in different periods' styles. There is also an exhibition by the British Toymakers Guild. Outside there is an attractive walled garden.

**Open:** 26th March to 30th October, Tuesday, Wednesday, Thursday, Saturday, Sunday and Good Friday, 2.00-6.00; Bank Holiday Mondays 12.00-6.00; Friday in July and August 2.00-6.00, Saturday and Sunday 12.00-6.00.

**Admission:** £3.50, child £1.50; garden £2.00, children free.

**Facilities:** Yorkshire recipes served in tearoom or the riverside tea garden. Car park. Shop.

**Disabled Access:** Ground floor only. Toilets.

**Additional information:** Picnics in car park. Dogs allowed in car park only.

**Special events:** There is a varied programme of events including a Christmas concert. There are also special exhibitions of prints, paintings, toys and model steam engines.

# TEMPLE NEWSAM HOUSE

*Leeds LS15 0AE Tel: (0532) 647321/641358*
*5m E of city centre, off A63*

**Ownership:** City of Leeds

**General Description:** Temple Newsam House is a magnificent Tudor-Jacobean mansion set in a 900 acre park laid out by 'Capability' Brown. It was the birthplace of Lord Darnley, husband of Mary Queen of Scots, and the home of the Ingram family until sold to Leeds by Lord Halifax in 1922. It contains a series of superb interiors ranging in style from the 16th to the 20th centuries, many recently restored using original wallcoverings and furniture. In them are collections of Old Master paintings, famous furniture by Thomas Chippendale, a large collection of Leeds creamware, and spectacular silver. The Park has celebrated rhododendrons and azaleas as well as a rose garden and an Italian garden. The workings of an agricultural estate and varieties of rare breeds of livestock can be seen at the Home Farm.

**Open:** All year Tuesday to Sunday and Bank Holiday Mondays, 10.30-5.30.

**Admission:** £2.00, concessions and child £1.00.

**Facilities:** The Stable Courtyard Café is open daily for coffee, lunch and tea. Car park. Shop.

**Disabled Access:** Limited access. Toilets.

**Additional information:** There will be two exhibitions – 'All that Glitters: Treasures of a Victorian Banker' and Miniature Furniture and Embroidery. Picnics in the park. Dogs allowed in park.

*The Great Hall*

# PICTURE ACKNOWLEDGEMENTS

The Publishers would like to acknowledge the following for permission to reproduce the pictures in this book:-

**Britain on View** - Front cover, Back cover, Dyrham Park, Woburn Abbey, Dorney Court, Ascott, Claydon House, Waddesdon Manor, Wimpole Hall, Little Morton Hall, Arley Hall, Gawsworth Hall, Dunham Massey Hall, St Michaels Mount, Lanhydrock, Levens Hall, Holker Hall, Dalemain, Haddon Hall, Hardwick Hall, Audley End House, The Banqueting House, Chiswick House, Hampton Court Palace (p 46), Kensington Palace, Kenwood, Kew Palace, Syon Park, Tower of London, Beaulieu Palace House, Stratfield Saye House, Berrington Hall, Knebworth House, Normanby Hall, Ightham Mote, Knole, Leighton Hall, Belton House, Sandringham House (p 90), Lamport Hall, Cragside House, Wallington House, Newstead Abbey, Milton Manor, Blenheim Palace (p 100), Montacute House, Ickworth House, Petworth House, Arbury Hall (p 119), Baddesley Clinton, Parkwood House, Ragley Hall, Wilton House, Beningborough Hall, Bramham Park, Harewood House (p 135), Castle Howard, Newby Hall, Temple Newsam House (p 142); **Britain on View - Brian Boyd** - Basildon Park, Chartwell, Boughton House, Polesden Lacey, Charlecote Park; **Britain on View - N. Holmes** - Cliveden, Blickling Hall, Felbrigg Hall, Oxburgh Hall, Canon Ashby House, Belsay Hall; **Britain on View - Barry Hicks** - Snowshill Manor; **Britain on View - Adam Woolfit** - Burton Agnes Hall, Holkham Hall; **Britain on View - Peter Cheze Brown** - Attingham Park; **Britain on View - W. Holmes** – Rufford Old Hall; **Mr Macleod Matthews** - Chenies Manor House; **North West Tourist Board** - Lyme Park, Croxteth Hall; **Mount Edgcumbe Country Park** - Mount Edgcumbe House; **Neil Jinkerson - Jarrold Colour Publications** - Mirehouse House; **Duke of Devonshire/Chatsworth House** - Chatsworth; **East Midlands Tourist Board** - Kedleston Hall; **East Midlands Tourist Board - Mike Williams** - Sudbury Hall; **Powderham Castle** - Powderham Castle; **Sherborne Castle - Holt Studios** - Sherborne Castle; **Woodmansterne** - Kingston Lacy (p 38); **National Trust** - Kingston Lacy (p 39), Ham House, Osterley Park, Clandon Park, Hatchlands Park, Loseley Park, Nunnington Hall; **London Tourist Board** - Buckingham Palace; **Royal Palaces** - Hampton Court Palace (p 47); **Lord Romsey** - Broadlands; **Terry Faragher** - The Vyne; **Hatfield House** - Hatfield House; **Sewerby Hall** - Sewerby Hall; **Osborne House** - Osborne House; **Penshurst Place** - Penshurst Place; **English Life Publications** - Belvoir Castle, Burghley House; **Stanford Hall** - Stanford Hall; **Ron Jones** - Speke Hall; **Sandringham Estate** - Sandringham House (p 91); **Blenheim Palace** - Blenheim Palace (p 101); **Stonor Park** - Stonor; **Weston Park** - Weston Park; **Shugborough Park** - The Shugborough Estate; **Parham** - Parham (p 114); **Highclere Castle** – Highclere Castle; **Walter Gardiner** - Parham (p 115); **The Royal Pavilion** - The Royal Pavilion; **Trans Globe Film Distribution** - Arbury Hall (p 118); **Bowood House** - Bowood House; **Longleat** - Longleat House; **Duncombe Park** - Duncombe Park; **East Riddlesden - P Wenham** - East Riddlesden Hall; **York Civic Trust** - Fairfax House; **Lotherton Hall** - Lotherton Hall; **Harewood House** - Harewood House (p 134); **Nostell Priory** - Nostell Priory; **Temple Newsam House** - Temple Newsam House (p 143).